Leadership, Violence, and School Climate

Case Studies in Creating Nonviolent Schools

Kyle E. Blanchfield and Peter D. Ladd

ROWMAN & LITTLEFIELD EDUCATION
A division of
ROWMAN & LITTLEFIELD PUBLISHERS, INC.
Lanham • New York • Toronto • Plymouth, UK

Published by Rowman & Littlefield Education
A division of Rowman & Littlefield Publishers, Inc.
A wholly owned subsidary of The Rowman & Littlefield Publishing Group, Inc.
4501 Forbes Boulevard, Suite 200, Lanham, Maryland 20706
www.rowman.com

10 Thornbury Road, Plymouth PL6 7PP, United Kingdom

British Library Cataloguing in Publication Information Available

Library of Congress Cataloging-in-Publication Data
Blanchfield, Kyle E.
Leadership, violence, and school climate : case studies in creating nonviolent schools / Kyle E. Blanchfield and Peter D. Ladd.
pages cm
Includes bibliographical references and index.
ISBN 978-1-4758-0170-5 (cloth : alk. paper)—ISBN 978-1-4758-0171-2 (pbk. : alk. paper)—ISBN 978-1-4758-0172-9 (electronic)
1. School violence—United States—Prevention. 2. School management and organization—United States. I. Ladd, Peter D. II. Title.
LB3013.32.B525 2013
371.7'820973—dc23
2013009109

∞™ The paper used in this publication meets the minimum requirements of American National Standard for Information Sciences Permanence of Paper for Printed Library Materials, ANSI/NISO Z39.48-1992.

Printed in the United States of America

We dedicate this book to those who seek the
reduction of violence in our schools.

Contents

Contents

Foreword

Mark Hyatt and Gregg Amore

In the wake of Sandy Hook Elementary School's searing intrusion into our collective national psyche, the timing of this important book could hardly be more urgent. As anyone who works in or around schools today knows, they are institutions vastly different from those we attended just decades ago. Schools at virtually every academic level have become a much more complex environment, with a diversity of issues, players, and threats that were simply not present when we were children, and with a wider array of issues comes greater opportunity for conflict. As a result, there is seemingly more violence—mental and physical—less respect, more isolation, and a dwindling sense of humanity and connectedness in too many of today's academic settings.

At St. Lawrence University in upstate New York, Drs. Kyle Blanchfield and Peter Ladd are two educators who know something about conflict resolution, having taught the subject for years while also acting as mediators, arbitrators, and third-party neutrals for all manner of disputes. In this book, drawing on that wide experience, they have created an effective resource that writes a clear prescription for achieving more democratic, nonviolent educational communities that are not only safer, but more conducive to student success. This work is a "must read" for every teacher who cares about creating that sort of classroom, where curiosity and learning trump fear and mistrust.

Conflict resolution in virtually any arena requires trust, fairness, engagement, and a general climate of respect, inclusion, and empowerment. The authors drive home this point with ten separate case studies that examine conflicts seemingly minor, others that wound up in court, and a few that made national news. Each offers its own valuable lesson in how important creating the proper school climate can be. Along the way, we see how helpful such underappreciated character traits as humor and generosity of spirit can be in defusing tension and preserving reason. Similarly, integrity and honesty breed trust, and as a result, students, parents, and teachers and administrators all feel more attuned to each other's needs.

The authors refer to this ideal as "democracy"—not where students vote on what's for lunch or whether or not to have homework—but where everyone in a school feels that they have actual worth and are empowered to improve themselves.

This positive *school culture and climate* naturally helps to reduce school violence, improve overall safety, and even boost grades. Indeed, the National School Climate Council believes such an affirming atmosphere fosters exactly the kind of youth development and learning necessary for a productive and satisfying life. If students feel socially, emotionally, and physically safe, then they are much more likely to become engaged in the process of their own education. In such a climate, educators actually teach better and parents even parent better. Students, families, and teachers work together to develop, live, and contribute to a shared school vision where learning once again is the only goal.

Schools with an intentional approach to creating caring, positive, democratic school cultures enable students to learn not only the academic skills they need to succeed but the personal skills they will also need—skills such as empathy for others, resiliency in the face of failure or adversity, and self-control. These skills can be fostered through a variety of research-based character education or social and emotional learning programs and practices. Blanchfield and Ladd realize all this and provide a richly detailed roadmap for achieving it.

Mark Hyatt
President and CEO
Character Education Partnerships
Washington, DC

Gregg Amore
Associate Dean of Students for Student Development
DeSales University
Center Valley, PA

Preface

Is it possible to reduce violence in our schools? This question can be debated not only from an individual school perspective, but also from the point of view of society, in general. The twenty-first century has brought numerous changes that make us more sophisticated communicators, enhanced information gatherers, and accessible to a way of life that can bring us closer together or tear us apart.

Violence is one phenomenon that has embraced the changes we now experience in the twenty-first century. For example, when violence strikes a school, such as in the massacre on December 14, 2012, in a Newtown, Connecticut, elementary school, many of us were affected by our ability to share in the horror, stay informed to the specifics, and to feel torn apart by the implications for our way of life. In trying to understand the question, whether it is possible to reduce violence in our schools, we must first assume the strong connection between violence and the changes made in our society.

Whether we live in a more violent age is debatable, but what cannot be debated is our accessibility to information that describes violence. Our accessibility to the experience of violence allows violent people an opportunity to make a dramatic and traumatic impact on the rest of us. An act of violence is no longer an isolated incident. It has become a shared experience.

Unfortunately, too many of our shared experiences with violence happen in schools. The anticipation, in some of us, regarding when the next school shooting will take place has changed school violence from an aberration to an expected event. Such events seem to be a chronic pattern that demands a response. From a school leadership perspective, this response can be found in the climate of a school. School leadership and school climate are intricately connected, especially when it pertains to violence in schools.

A return to the basic concepts of democracy describes our response for reducing school violence. We believe it is the responsibility of our leaders to practice and restore democracy not only in the climate of our schools, but in the climate of our society. We are in an age where the experience of violence needs a more holistic and multidimensional response, and democracy is the response that changes the environment where violence takes place.

Violence does not happen in a vacuum. It diminishes or increases according to the climate where it exists. Democratic principles restore a way of life based on sharing the burden of violence, not being torn apart by it. The phenomenon of violence in the twenty-first century can be challenged by practicing "democracy," and that includes the practice of democracy in our schools.

The information in the following chapters is our attempt at answering the question "Is it possible to reduce violence in our schools?" The question is based on the belief that the emotional climate found in schools has similar characteristics to the emotional climate found in our society. In other words, what we experience in our schools represents the mood, attitude, beliefs, and behavior of our society. In this book, *Leadership, Violence and School Climate: Case Studies in Creating Nonviolent Schools*, we emphasize three important themes: democratic leadership, violence, and school climate. We believe all three need consideration in reducing school violence.

However, this requires school leaders to go beyond the skills needed for effective administration. It requires an understanding of the tenets found in democracy, and recognition of how closely democratic leadership is connected to the climate found in schools. Principles of democracy are covered in the book, such as empowerment, assertiveness, common ground, generosity, and others, along with methods of intervention when a school experiences emotional, psychological, and physical violence, crisis, and trauma.

The question of how to reduce violence in schools is answered, in part, by putting democracy back in schools, especially into the school climate. It is the climate of our schools that reflects and is influenced by the mood of our society. In the twenty-first century, we have an opportunity to influence not only our society, but also our schools. Some of the methods for accomplishing the reduction of violence in schools will come from outside experts.

We look to experts from outside of schools to develop innovative methods and skills that address specific issues such as mental health issues, teacher training, lockdowns, or more sophisticated instruments to detect possible violence such as metal detectors and enhanced security systems. We also look to our politicians for solutions such as gun control, while protecting Second Amendment civil liberties.

Beyond such advances and political issues remains a more subtle yet powerful phenomenon at work that directly has an impact on school leadership. Specific methods for reducing violence in our schools are temporary

unless we change the underlying sources of violence. Returning to the principles of democracy addresses one of these underlying sources. The emotional
climate of our society may be ready for a return to democratic principles that
counteract violence, while improving the emotional climate of its schools.

This book is dedicated to that end. As educators, we realize the following
chapters will not supply all the answers to the complex phenomenon of
school violence. Yet it is our contribution from a school leadership perspective concerning an issue that leaves us restless and unsatisfied. Is it possible
to reduce violence in our schools? We hope the following information will
help in answering this timely yet complex question.

Kyle E. Blanchfield and Peter D. Ladd
St. Lawrence University
January 6, 2013

Acknowledgments

We would like to thank those people who inspired the case studies found in this book. We changed specific names and locations in each case study in order to protect the anonymity of those willing to help us. However, it is important to note that practicing democracy in a healthy school climate is not just an idea but a real-life practice.

We would like to thank the institutions described in chapter 12 for their belief in democratic leadership and their commitment to an effective school climate. In this regard, we want to acknowledge Linda Zerbe, dean of students, and Gregg Amore, associate dean of students for student development at DeSales University, for their expertise regarding school climate at the university level.

Acknowledgment goes out to Rod Cook, director of the higher education program on the Akwesasne Mohawk Reservation, for his commitment to the education of Native people, and for his tireless effort in keeping diversity a major priority for teachers, students, and school leaders. Acknowledgment also goes out to those people who practice and commit themselves to Native culture, where many of the ideas found in this book developed meaning and identity.

Acknowledgments go out to Mark Hyatt, president and CEO of Character Education Partnerships, for his belief in empowerment and a democratic form of leadership. His efforts have helped hundreds of public schools understand a more balanced approach to education, where human development has equal importance with academic achievement. We also thank Mark for his commitment to the human development of student character. We believe his understanding of this issue is in the forefront of progressive ideas in education.

We would like to thank Jonathan Cohen, president and CEO of the National School Climate Center, for the research he and others have done in the area of school climate, and for the help and guidance he has given the authors of this book. Without the efforts of the National School Climate Center, important and viable research would not be available to those professionals who believe in democratic principles in schools.

Chapter One

Overview

To educate a man in mind and not in morals is to educate a menace to society.

—Theodore Roosevelt

The debate continues as to what constitutes an effective leader in today's schools. Some experts assume that leadership in schools requires effective management skills, while others believe that leaders need a vision and philosophy that gives direction and purpose to a school's everyday functioning (Shouppe and Pate 2010). This book embraces both concepts, where being a leader and manager come together through the principles found in a more democratic leadership style. However, regarding school management, this book will focus more on how to manage the climate of a school and the people in it, especially concerning the management of school-related violence.

Also, you will find that the definition of democratic leadership in this book includes not only "top-down" methods of leading others. It defines leadership as "anyone in a school who has a vision for making the school better," again with an emphasis on addressing violence in schools. Most important, this is a book about developing a shared vision of how to create nonviolent schools, where principles of democracy are practiced, and where the school climate is an expression of nonviolence rather than violence.

DEMOCRACY AND LEADERSHIP

What are the characteristics of a more democratic leadership style? One of the first tenets of democracy coincides with democratic leadership found in this book. Both make the statement that values the importance of having a shared vision. In other words, a vision of how to become successful is collaborative, where all involved accept ownership for the vision. For example, a vision for how to create a nonviolent school climate is understood and practiced by all those involved in making such a vision successful.

Researchers have stated that many of today's schools are some of the *least democratic* institutions (Browne 2012). However, we may have entered an era where the sharing of information through networking, and other examples from our information age, have given credence to sharing a collective vision, one where all involved are empowered to facilitate growth and change.

A vision of democratic school leadership also may need the skills to communicate that vision to others. Research shows that effective school leaders possess not only management skills, but also the language of self-expression (Manasse 1986). Leaders who cannot effectively communicate with others or network such a vision may diminish their effectiveness. For democratic leaders, this becomes the ability to communicate beyond faculty and staff. A democratic style of leadership demands a vision that is successfully communicated to faculty, staff, students, parents, the community, and other professional organizations, where all involved understand and share a similar vision of the school.

In order to effectively communicate the vision of a school, democratic leaders are more people oriented (Donaldson 2006). We hear the term *people oriented* in numerous management styles of school leadership, but what does the term mean? From a democratic perspective, *people oriented* means empowering others, so all involved can represent a school's vision. It is where a consensus of opinion can influence one person's opinion. People oriented also means having a certain loyalty to the school's leadership. Here is where being a self-centered or self-serving leader diminishes the shared vision of a school.

One example applies to a major theme found in this book. People oriented may involve collaborating on the most effective methods for creating a nonviolent school climate. In this regard, *people oriented* means creating common ground between school personnel where they share beliefs, procedures, resources, and consequences.

More democratic leaders also embrace diversity and difference, where achievement alone does not determine success in schools (Dimmock and Walker 2005). It is a leadership style where people are honored for their uniqueness as well as rewarded for their achievement. As defined in the principles of democracy, more democratic leaders believe in the equal rights of others. In today's achievement-oriented school climate, only rewarding those who academically succeed may be one of the criteria leading to violence in schools. In democratic leadership, honoring school personnel for their individual differences becomes as important as rewarding people for doing what they are told.

Democracy in schools is not only the result of following the rules. It requires generosity, where all involved feel a part of something shared together. It works from the assumption that "the whole is bigger than the sum of its parts." In other words, all people in the school are as important as any one person, and where diversity enriches the school rather than polarizing it. In an age where violence in schools has become a focal point of discussion, democratic school leadership may hold more hope in reducing the characteristics associated with this problem.

LEADERSHIP AND SCHOOL CLIMATE

Beyond creating a more democratic leadership style in schools is the climate where such leadership can grow and change. A school's climate can be defined as the traditions, beliefs, policies, norms, and practiced skills that act as a foundation for what takes place within the everyday workings of a school (Cohen et al. 2009). It also means the experience of being in a school where policies, norms, and practices take place (Cohen et al. 2009). All styles of leadership create a foundation that affects the behavior of everyone associated with a school. In this regard, leadership roles in schools need a clear understanding of the foundation being created and its effects on the school climate.

Regarding the foundation of democratic school leaders, it is the reciprocal relationship between democratic leadership and the type of climate found in the school that defines the success or failure of both concepts within this foundation. For example, democratic leadership in a climate of oppression probably will not work. Democracy requires empowerment rather than force. It requires valuing the importance of school climate in sharing a vision or in making change.

Regarding violence in schools, it also requires a shift in thinking that may improve the chances for having a nonviolent school. A negative school climate can become one of the breeding grounds for developing violence in schools, where a positive school climate can engender nonviolence and cooperation, not polarization. The following are a brief introduction to those elements needed in creating a nonviolent school climate, all found within the foundation of a democratic style of leadership. In the next ten chapters these elements will be more fully discussed, but for now, consider the following themes when creating a nonviolent school climate:

Crisis

Crisis in schools can range from natural disasters, neighborhood and community violence, or internal violence through gossiping, bullying, and sabotaging the vision of schools. In order for schools to formally be in crisis, it requires school leaders to recognize those suffering from the crisis and how their suffering diminishes school performance. Disasters such as the shooting at Sandy Hook Elementary School and other similar dramatic news stories make crisis easy to recognize.

However, how does school leadership define crisis when it is subtle and less pronounced? Bullying, forms of discrimination, harassment, and others may fall under the radar of an unobservant school leader who is focusing exclusively on management rather than what is happening in the climate of the school. Without understanding how crisis impacts school climate, school leaders run the risk of not recognizing when it is happening to school personnel.

They also run the risk of *not realizing* its impact on the functioning of a school. Crisis can have a devastating impact on a school's success. By understanding crisis in schools the saying "with crisis comes opportunity for change" may be a crucial opportunity for democratic leadership to make change through crisis resolution. Preparing for an eventual crisis may include engaging school personnel in a collaborative effort to avoid crisis, rather than only intervening when a crisis takes place. Also, crisis can have devastating consequences to the climate of a school, or it can be viewed as an opportunity to improve the school climate while preparing for future crises.

Trauma

The recent reports of school shootings, bullying, and other forms of lateral violence in schools has created a mind-set where dealing with trauma may be a part of any school leader's job description. This does not mean school leadership needs to take the place of psychologists, psychiatrists, and school counselors when dealing with school trauma. These professionals are trained in the treatment of individual trauma and its impact on people within the school.

It means that contemporary leaders in schools need an understanding of the effects of trauma on the school climate. Ultimately, it will be school leadership that either learns from the trauma in order to make people in the school more resilient and productive or allows school-related trauma to freeze productivity in a school in the aftermath. Facing trauma in today's schools may be another mandate for a more democratic form of leadership.

Working through trauma may be the responsibility of its leaders, where avoidance of trauma can have devastating effects on schools. One only has to use the example of the sexual trauma experienced in the 2011 crisis at Penn State University to recognize just how long it takes for a school climate to heal after school leaders practice avoidance of trauma. In more democratic forms of leadership, the school climate becomes as important as the individual intentions of its leaders. Working through trauma for the common good becomes one of the tenets found in successful democracy in schools.

Emotions

An understanding of key emotions in a school setting can set the tone for more positive responses when school personnel are in conflict. For example, when people become angry in a school, this may not be the time to establish new rules and regulations. It may be important for disputing parties to vent, and when the anger passes, only then address changes in school procedures. Many schools prematurely jumping to create "zero tolerance" are an example of reactionary policies rather than thought-out procedures (Kafka 2011).

There is a window of opportunity facing school leaders when anger infiltrates the climate of a school. Trying to resolve it too soon gives little time for reason to return for an effective resolution. Trying to resolve it too late results in either people in the school resolving it for themselves without including others or turning their anger into resentment, where they can indirectly lash out at others through forms of lateral violence.

For ineffective school leaders, dealing with angry disputes can result in judging or avoiding effective methods for conflict resolution. In more democratic leadership, resolving angry disputes may be more productive than dealing with the resentment created by judgments or avoidance of these disputes. Resentment or civilized anger in schools finds its solution through gossiping, blaming, and complaining. People in schools have less trouble giving up their problems than giving up their solutions to their problems. Practicing resentment is a solution to being angry, and school leadership may need to understand the difficulty in removing resentment from a school climate.

Empowerment

"Who has the power?" is an unavoidable question when considering school climate—the power to make decisions, discuss problems, share beliefs, complete tasks, and many others. Empowerment in the climate of a school is not about school leadership giving others power by creating a hierarchy of "power brokers" in schools. Ironically, this can lead to an imbalance of power, where conflict develops through jealousy, resentment, and protection of one's "turf." Empowerment is creating an atmosphere where people feel that they can "empower themselves." Empowerment in schools is based on the democratic principle that people have the right to express personal growth and change.

A climate of empowerment in schools can lessen school-related conflict and possible violence (Richardson, Lane, and Flanigan 1995). Many school-related disputes are based on a loss of empowerment, where feelings of oppression become more important than the specifics associated with a dispute. For example, if someone is given extra tasks to perform, it may be the lack of discussion about doing these tasks, not the tasks themselves, that will make another feel oppressed or disempowered. Keeping this in mind, a democratic leader may have to empower people in a dispute by helping them resolve their problems among themselves.

Assertiveness

Assertiveness appears to be one of the fundamental communication skills needed in establishing a climate of democracy in schools and in resolving school-related conflict. Assertiveness is primarily about advocating for yourself through clear expressions of your point of view. Yet assertiveness is more than clearly expressing yourself. It also includes respecting the rights of others and knowing that what is expressed has an impact on them. Being assertive is not only about what you have to say, but also "how you say it." Unfortunately, many school-related disputes go unresolved when school leaders do not use assertive communication.

In a climate of oppression, school-related conflict is more frequently addressed with aggressive, passive, or passive/aggressive communication (Ladd 2005). During a school dispute, communication may become so aggressive that disputing parties become offended and shut down. Other times, the dispute can become so passive that an "illusion of harmony" takes place, where people smile at each other while the dispute simmers just under the surface. Other times the dispute can be placed on the workplace "grapevine," where outsiders can join in through gossip, backbiting, and other forms of indirect lashing out. More democratic leaders know the value of assertive communication, where they help people in the dispute be proactive rather than reactive, where they can express themselves and do not hurt others.

Common Ground

Many school leaders were taught that in order to be effective problem solvers when people are in conflict, it is important to isolate the differences between people or groups by weighing facts and making accurate judgments. Unfortunately, this practice does not work well when disputing parties are affecting the climate of a school. In disputes concerning school climate, isolating facts and making judgments may continue to polarize an already polarized situation. What may be needed is the art of finding common ground between people.

Reestablishing what people have in common reduces the distance between polarized people or groups. It helps "shrink" the dispute to a workable level based on the assumption. The more common ground established in a dispute, the less issues needing resolution. More effective, democratic school leaders establish common ground in schools in order to lessen school violence while increasing growth and change.

Humor

There are different functions for using humor in the climate of a school setting beyond creating laughter and amusement. Humor can act as an effective coping mechanism when school-related conflict begins to reach a critical stage. Humor can make a school setting more relaxed, manageable, enjoyable, and interesting. Humor can be most effective in preventing conflict as a nonthreatening intervention, when direct or indirect violence takes place. One of the benefits of using humor in a school is its remarkable ability to reduce stress.

Humor can also reduce the power imbalances between people while expanding the boundaries of what is a possible resolution when dealing with violence in schools. Democratic leadership in schools may use humor in highly stressed disputes to help create motivation and teamwork. Humor can be the common ground needed for people in schools to tolerate each other's differences and to productively continue on in spite of these differences. More important, *humor is as contagious as violence.* Both can spread quickly. More democratic leaders recognize humor as a valuable ingredient in spreading a climate of good will across a school that suffers from the violent acts of others.

Critical Thinking

Critical thinking in schools can be defined as a thoughtful, open-minded approach to problem solving, where resolution is based on the accuracy found in the arguments and opinions of effective leadership, and other critical thinkers in schools. Critical thinking involves accurate reasoning and honesty, while considering all possibilities and eliminating biases. However, a critical thinker is able to admit a lack of understanding, and adjust a point of view, when new information is found to be more accurate. Critical thinking may cease to exist when people have polarized into groups of "us against them."

When conflict has polarized the school climate, critical thinking can be replaced with "black-and-white" thinking or with an "us against them" mentality. At this point, school conflict becomes, "Who is to blame?" (black-and-white thinking), rather than identification of the problem or dispute (critical thinking). People begin talking "at" each other, not "to" each other, sometimes defending their positions at all costs. More democratic school leadership has a mandate to reestablish critical thinking when trying to resolve conflict in schools. Without a sense of collaborative dialogue, black-and-white thinking may cause disputing parties to blame each other for extended periods of time.

Generosity

We probably know of school climates that have become self-centered and self-serving, where greed seems more the norm than acts of generosity. Yet what we may not know is the impact such a negative experience has on increasing conflict in schools. By sharing ideas, opinions, and differing points of view, more democratic school leaders not only allow for conflicting opinions, but also for a climate of generosity to form within the group. Generosity creates a sense of accessibility to each other, where people in the school can engage in conflict resolution, even when they agree to disagree.

A lack of generosity by those in the climate of a school can create win/lose outcomes when people are in conflict. That may be why mediation and conciliation procedures have become more practiced methods in resolving school-related disputes (Cohen 1999). One of the ground rules for engaging in these practices is that disputing parties are allowed to share their points of view, equally. In this manner, disputing parties become accessible to each other, while giving credibility to opposing points of view. A lack of generosity has the opposite effect, where people in dispute are not accessible to each other, and where their points of view can easily be dismissed for lacking credibility.

Trust

Trust may be the "glue" needed in schools that keeps interpersonal relationships cohesive and alive. This becomes an even greater issue when people have a problem surrounding the climate of the school, such as when there are rumors about the dependability of an administrator. Usually, trust in schools begins by its leaders reaching out to others, and engaging them in an authentic manner. This may be why creating dialogue in schools becomes such an important concept to grasp by more democratic leadership. However, trust is solidified after a school conflict has been resolved, when people in the school remain dependable and genuine in the resolution of the conflict.

The issue of trust and its relationship to school climate is most consistently in jeopardy when people do not share their intentions with others. Hidden agendas, secrecy, and only sharing intentions with a select few erodes a sense of trust. Transparency by school leadership creates a sense of loyalty toward common goals. Lack of transparency has a devastating impact on how much people are willing to trust each other. One of the goals of successful democratic leaders is to reach out to others with the goal of transparency, which helps to establish trust.

LEADERSHIP AND SCHOOL VIOLENCE

The case studies found in this book reflect different forms of violence in schools but also address how democratic leaders practice either prevention or intervention in resolving violence. Some of the case studies discuss topics such as bullying, sexual abuse, suicide, school-related shootings, violence through drug use, and numerous others. They approach violence not only from a physical perspective, but also from an emotional and psychological point of view.

The case studies also address contemporary trends in preventing violence in schools: zero tolerance policies, the use of metal detectors, and locker searches. In all of these themes, a more democratic leadership style is applied for the reduction or prevention of violence and the creation of nonviolent schools.

When taking into consideration that 77 percent of all students in schools have experienced some form of bullying, including mentally, verbally, and physically (U.S. Department of Justice 2012), having school leaders address school violence may be as big an issue as school budgets or curriculum. It also may be important to point out the "ripple effect" of such acts as bullying or harassment in schools. For example, young people who bully others are more likely to smoke, drink, and get into fights with others. Such a ripple effect can begin with verbal bullying behaviors that go unnoticed by school leaders, and eventually escalate into the potential for school shootings.

During 2009–2010 there were eleven deaths due to school violence, with revenge being the strongest motivating factor (U.S. Department of Justice 2012). In a more democratic style of leadership, the "ripple effect" of escalating violence becomes a matter of prevention rather than intervention. That is why seven chapters in the book address prevention, while three chapters address what happens when violence is not prevented. The final chapter describes programs where these themes take place.

Leadership, violence, and school climate are the overriding themes found in the book. They reflect a democratic form of leadership where school leaders have a vision and share that vision with other members of the school community. It also is a book that values the importance in maintaining a nonviolent school climate, where empowerment, common ground, assertiveness, critical thinking, and other important skills make up the expertise needed in maintaining a shared vision. The following chapters include discussions pertaining to violence and nonviolence. Through the use of case studies it is hoped that readers will develop an understanding of the subtleties and nuances of violence beyond the drama of tragic yet dramatic violent events such as school shootings.

The reality is that most violent acts that take place in schools do not result in fatalities. They are the everyday acts of violence that have the potential to escalate into fatalities so often covered in the media. When someone associated with a school has lost reason and decides to retaliate against others, it may begin with an accumulation of small acts of violence. The ability to create nonviolent schools may neutralize the drama found in serious violent acts. Nonviolent schools can benefit from democratic leaders, where the climate of the school is valued along with other leadership responsibilities. This also includes democratic principles that help school leaders work in preventing violence, while being prepared to intervene if or when violence happens in the school.

Part I

Intervention

Chapter Two

Crisis

If you were to define crisis in a school what comes to mind? Does your definition include natural disasters, suicides, bullying, fighting, or possibly indirect violence happening around a school, such as violence in a neighboring community? Though all of these events have similar characteristics based on some form of trauma, they do not necessarily constitute a crisis. Certain elements must be present in order for school leaders to assess that a crisis is taking place. The traumatic event alone does not necessarily mean a school is experiencing a crisis.

Beyond the event itself are two other factors that constitute a crisis for school leaders; namely, does the leadership perceive that people are suffering from the experience, and does the leadership perceive their suffering is caus-

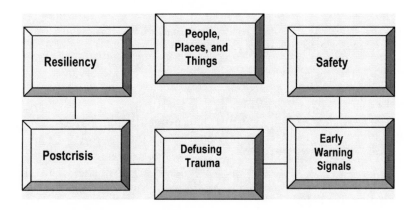

Figure 2.1.   An Outline for Crisis

ing diminished performance beyond typical coping mechanisms expected in everyday conflict (Jackson-Cherry and Erford 2010).

When two students shot and killed school personnel and fellow students at Columbine High School in 1999, all three elements were present: a traumatic event, perceived suffering, and the diminished performance (or no performance) by the members of the school, which was caused by the suffering. The school was shocked, causing severe difficulty in coping with the crisis situation (McKenry and Price 2005).

Another example that corresponds to our definition of crisis occurred on April 14, 2007, when Seung-Hui Cho victimized thirty-two people at Virginia Tech. Beyond the obvious trauma was the valiant effort by police and emergency personnel to save lives and manage crisis found in this tragic disaster. However, despite the bravery of emergency response personnel, questions surfaced regarding school leadership and their response to the perceived suffering of others (Lazenby 2007).

In the following chapter, we will address the fundamental ingredients needed by school leaders in making an accurate crisis intervention response. As stated above, beyond any tragic incident in school is the perception of crisis, how much suffering is experienced, and how the crisis has diminished the ability of staff and students to continue learning with a sense of normalcy. Added to these three characteristics are safety issues that become a major concern for anyone involved in school crisis and how effective school leaders are at creating a safe environment during these crises. Early warning signals for potential crisis are included along with defusing the trauma associated with crisis intervention.

Furthermore, it may be equally important how leaders effectively deal with the climate of the school postcrisis, and how resilient the school is in facing crisis in the future. Though crisis intervention for school leaders may include specific techniques, general concepts of democratic leadership may also be important in understanding effective crisis intervention where honor, respect, and credibility become indirect consequences of effective leadership during and after a crisis (Bockler et al. 2012).

CASE STUDY

This case study begins on a negative note. It includes a twelfth-grade star football player at a suburban school, the school's high school principal and football coach, and an eleventh-grade female student from the same school. The crisis incident took place during the height of the football season, where a party was taking place after a decisive win for the home school.

Drugs and alcohol were everywhere, and the star player had cornered the eleventh-grade female student in the backyard where the party was taking place. Despite her protests, he was able to forcibly make explicit and physical sexual overtures, and he continued to do so until he returned to the celebration, while she found herself walking, crying, and having feelings of rage until she reached the safety of her own home.

The next day she and her parents filed charges against the male perpetrator for sexual harassment, and they had an order of protection granted by the court, where the male student was found guilty of the charge. However, the high school principal/football coach convinced the girl's parents that she should be the student who would remain at home, and for a short period of time they complied with the principal's decision. However, this did not solve the problem.

Beyond the sexual harassment charges was another crisis facing the school community. The incident had polarized the school into two camps: one for the female student's part of the crisis, and the other for the crisis that supported the male student and the decision of the principal. At this point, the school was in crisis, and someone was needed who could administer some form of crisis intervention.

All heads turned to the school superintendent to give direction to the crisis, and it was the superintendent who became the arbitrator, mediator, and judge in finding a reasonable resolution. The first step was to uphold the law and honor the order of protection. Yet this was complicated based on the principal's decision that the sexual harassment victim remain at home, while the perpetrator continued in classes and as a star player on the football team. Safety became a paramount concern based on the friction growing between the opposing groups of supporters at the school. The superintendent recognized that the crisis had spread to include the emotional climate of the school, where the climate was ripe for collateral and escalating crises to occur.

The superintendent needed a crisis intervention plan that met all of the elements of this particular crisis, namely, resolution for the legal aspects pertaining to the school, safety for the harassment victim and the people in the school climate, and a plan that did not violate the right of any student who wanted to go to school. The first step was to present the following proposal to the school board. The following crisis intervention plan was presented and approved:

- Ask the judge that the order of protection be modified so that both parties could attend school. (This request was granted.)
- Have the guidance counselor responsible for scheduling classes and lunchroom periods alter the schedules of both students so that minimal contact is possible. (The schedules were changed.)
- Have the judge approve a one-time meeting between the two students for victim/offender mediation, and bring in an outside mediator to mediate between the victim and the perpetrator in this crisis. (This is where the

offender of an incident must face his or her victim and discuss reconciliation in the presence of a neutral, third-party mediator. The judge agreed
and the mediation was successful.)
• Place a letter of reprimand in the file of the principal based on violating
the legal rights of a student to a public school education. (Reprimand
accepted.)

Though the superintendent's plan was not perfect, and grumblings of the
incident took time before they finally ended, it appeared the school had
returned to a sense of normalcy. For the most part, people connected to the
crisis felt the intervention was fair and balanced, with the possible exception
of the high school principal.

CRISIS AND SCHOOL CLIMATE

People, Places, and Things

The field of education is filled with different risk factors that may increase
the need for leaders to consider some form of crisis intervention. For example, any time a workplace has to make judgments or enforce some form of
disciplinary code, the potential for crisis intervention needs consideration.
Schools are run on such procedures that require judgments such as disciplinary codes, judgments on grades, making judgments on student placement,
dress codes, drug and alcohol, codes based on truancy, judgments during
performance appraisals, judgments regarding which students or staff appear
psychologically stable and which do not, and many others (Knoff 2012;
Larrivee 2012).

Furthermore, schools are usually found in community-based settings
where crisis may spread to the school or may spill over into the community
once a school crisis has taken place—for example, school shootings, students
in car accidents, or student suicides. Beyond specific situations, schools may
experience crisis at certain times of the day, night, or year. After-school
hours or early morning before the start of school are periods of transition
where crisis is more likely to happen, or during report card periods or parent/
teacher conferences.

School leaders also must consider crises that are out of their control, such
as natural disasters or economic cutbacks. The risk of crisis intervention may
happen depending on geographic location—for example, buildings or busi-
nesses that are at risk for violent crime such as banks, bars, or liquor stores.
As it turns out, crisis intervention begins with people, places, and things.

Effective Leadership

In the case study, all three elements of people, places, and things were in-cluded in the crisis facing the superintendent of the school. The students directly involved in the crisis, the parents of these students, and the people within the school all had an investment in the resolution of this crisis. Places also needed consideration: where the law was clear that people within a certain age group (usually up to twenty-one years old) have a right to attend public school and cannot be denied that right, the superintendent considered specific things. In this case, the volatility connected to a crisis where sexual and other forms of harassment were perceived as taking place between stu-dent/student, but also in this case, between student/principal.

All of these elements need consideration when developing a crisis inter-vention plan, where the leader does not underestimate the breadth and depth of the crisis. Finally, the case study brings up the "ripple effect" of indirect crisis emanating from the original crisis. The superintendent may also want to consider the long-term effects of decisions made during crisis, and how they may be viewed as discriminatory or prejudiced, as in the principal's decision to arbitrarily send the female student home without consideration to what effect such a decision would have on the climate of the school.

Safety

In crisis situations, probably the most important issue is the safety of the entire school community. This is especially true with those crises where physical safety concerns dominate the nature of the crisis. As school leaders, it becomes paramount that the warning signs are recognized by staff mem-bers and reported to the person in charge. Warning signs such as a history of violent behavior, psychiatric or forensic history, intoxication, erratic speech and behavior, sexual posturing and insinuation, and stalking are a few of the most common reported signs in schools. Most important, the leader or staff members need to pay attention to their "gut feelings" when reporting these crises.

Here are other important questions to ask when considering crisis inter-vention: "Do you have a mechanism to call for help?" "Are there areas set up as an escape route for others in the school if violence occurs?" "Do you have safety rules, and do people in the school abide by them?" All of these help protect the safety of the people who might find themselves in the middle of a school crisis.

Effective leaders should be prepared for implementing safety procedures rather than overreacting when a crisis occurs. In understanding any school climate, one must consider whether a school is safe. However, it may be important for school leaders to define safety more holistically beyond mere physical safety. For example, even when people in the school are physically safe, do they *feel* safe? It may be that peoples' perception of safety is as important as their physical safety.

Effective Leadership

In the case study, the rationale for the principal removing the harassed student was based on her physical safety. However, defining safety in any crisis as only physical safety may underestimate people's perception of safety. The case study exemplifies this point. In the case study, the decision to send the female home for her physical safety polarized the people in the school, making them perceive the school as an unsafe place.

When a school becomes polarized into groups and loses its common ground, the possibility for further conflict exists (Cherry and Spiegel 2006). In the case study, the superintendent took a more holistic approach to safety, and considered not only the physical safety of the school, but also in reestablishing a more emotionally safe school environment. Leaders in schools may want to consider a more expanded and holistic view of keeping their schools safe.

Early Warning Signals

Crisis intervention may require school leaders to be proactive, not reactive. There are specific warning signals often demonstrated before certain crises occur in the climate of a school. These may appear obvious to some, but they are worth citing as points of clarification:

- People who make either direct or veiled verbal threats of harm, or by making predictions of bad things to come.
- Being a loner with little involvement with other students or staff.
- Being overinvolved with others. For example, overinvolvement leading to issues of sexual harassment.
- Not being able to take criticism well. This can be focused on staff as well, where being judged becomes personal to the point of taking action.
- Pushing the limits of school safety beyond normal conduct with a history of violent behavior that continuously goes beyond the boundaries of school rules.
- Having an obsessive involvement with paramilitary training, weapons collections, and concealed weapons.
- A person having constant feelings of panic and overexaggeration of everyday conflict, where there are perceptions that the whole world is against the person.

Though some of these may appear obvious, this list was compiled from actual accounts of school trauma, where a school leader missed one or more of these points of clarification (Newman et al. 2005).

Effective Leadership

Though most of the above points do not pertain to the case study in this chapter, there are warning signals that have received serious scrutiny in today's public schools and universities, namely, overinvolvement or inappropriate involvement. The current media is filled with such stories of teacher/ student intimate relationships, sexual scandals, and what is seen as school professional/student overinvolvement. In the case study, it appeared that the principal's decision to send the female student home and retain the male student was an example of overinvolvement, or at least inappropriate involvement.

The saying "as a teacher or administrator you can be friendly to students but you are not their friends" may apply in this case. The principal lost sight of the camaraderie of being a coach, and the responsibility of being a school leader. It may be the responsibility of school leaders to be aware of signals that warn against such boundary crossings.

In the case study, we credit the superintendent with recognizing the principal's overinvolvement with the football player and the inappropriate decision that was made. There is a fine line between having a school climate based on such variables as empathy, empowerment, humor, and trust, and one based on inappropriate variables, such as intimacy, favoritism, or friendships.

Defusing Trauma

Responding to trauma is the emotional part of any crisis intervention and becomes the leader's emotional response for insuring safety and dealing with people, places, and things. One of the first steps leaders may consider is how trauma heightens peoples' emotions and speeds up the pace of almost anyone in the climate of the school. Pacing here simply means breathing more slowly and talking more slowly, while lowering one's tone of voice so that others will follow your lead. School leaders may initially need to pace a group of traumatized people down to a level where they can respond more logically.

Safety concerns are better handled when people have calmed down. In the same vein, leaders may consider reframing what people are saying and feeling in a more reasonable manner. For example, try to reframe the word *crisis* by referring to it as the *incident*. Or, as in the case study, change the topic away from references dealing with sexual harassment, toward references pertaining to a student's right to an education (Moore et al., 2011). Here are other specific pointers in helping to defuse school trauma:

- Be an empathic listener and a tactful responder to people in crisis.
- Being respectful helps others who are experiencing panic, or other forms of feeling out of control.
- Form bonds or connections even with those where there were no past bonds or connection, such as a leader bonding with students who have just witnessed a school shooting.
- Try to be reassuring by breaking the crisis down into manageable talking points. For example, if someone gets hurt, discuss immediate procedures for crisis intervention before discussions of any changes in procedures when the crisis is over.
- Focus on calming yourself down before trying to calm others down.
- During a crisis, do not make false statements or promises you cannot keep. For example, "Everybody calm down. Things will be all right."
- Try *not* to minimize the seriousness of the situation. People will decide for themselves how serious they believe the crisis is for them.
- Try not to take sides or agree with false information pertaining to the crisis.

Probably one of the most important messages in responding to crisis is that you will be in charge: have a plan for helping people either work through the crisis, or a plan to help them recover after the crisis is over.

Effective Leadership

In the case study, the superintendent made a statement that the crisis in the school was more than making a judgment based on the order of protection. As a leader, there was an effort to consider the trauma experienced by the girl when ordering victim/offender mediation. Leaders may consider that any crisis emanating from a conflict has two crucial elements. The first is the facts pertaining to the conflict. In the case study, the superintendent was keen to point out that the principal was not following the public school mandate in offering the girl the right to a public school education.

The second was acknowledgment of the trauma by offering her victim/offender mediation. In other words, a conflict is a combination of facts and feelings, and resolving facts alone may not be grounds for effective leadership, especially if negative feelings of one person in crisis can spread through the emotional climate of a school. More democratic school leaders may step beyond being an administrator when crisis hits the school. Democratic leaders may be the key professionals who are responsible for controlling trauma as well as crisis intervention procedures.

Postcrisis

Crises have a beginning, middle, and an end. If they do not end then school leaders are faced with another problem based on the crisis remaining in the climate of the school. This can dramatically change the unspoken rules inherent in any school climate. For example, people who used to talk to each other are now cautious of talking to each other, or people who previously shared opinions and feelings with the administration stop sharing. Such changes in the unspoken rules of a school climate are coping mechanisms that do not help to end a crisis.

In some ways, schools that are coping with the fallout of a crisis are as vulnerable as schools in crisis. Even though the crisis issues are less evident, it does not mean they are not having a dramatic impact on the school climate. Some school leaders make the mistake of acting as though a crisis is over without creating emotional closure, and leave people in the school to cope as best they can. Unfortunately, coping with previous trauma can happen for long periods of time. School leaders need an awareness of how people are coping and what impact the crisis is having on the climate itself. In democratic leadership, the climate of an institution may be as important as the people in it.

Effective Leadership

Coping with crisis can spread beyond the boundaries of a school. In the case study, the sexual harassment charges did not happen at school, but the emotional fallout from the incident became a crisis for school leadership. Sometimes, the solution to a crisis can be more disruptive than the crisis itself. The case study is an example of leadership that initially did not consider the climate of the school, but impulsively rushed in making a judgment that polarized the school community. A school community in crisis may be more adaptable when consideration is given to what is expected in the climate of the school, combined with crisis intervention procedures.

Only responding to the crisis itself without consideration of the fallout it may generate postcrisis can appear as leadership incompetence, even when leaders accurately react to crisis. In the case study, the principal solved the order of protection problem for the school but created another crisis in such a resolution. The superintendent took a more democratic approach, and looked for a solution that considered not only the incident, but also the climate of the school.

Resiliency

Leaders that are aware and practice safety issues, along with an understanding of issues surrounding school crises, may be in a better position to go beyond coping with the crisis and can establish a more resilient school climate after the crisis is over. Such leadership becomes a dynamic show of expertise in a crisis situation where more than ending the crisis or coming up with new rules of behavior is at stake. Beyond intervening in any given crisis is the ability to help others adapt after the crisis is over. Resiliency can be the final reward for leaders and schools that successfully work through and eventually learn from a crisis situation. The message sent to the school is: "We work through crisis" or "We do not react to crisis."

How many stories have we read about where a school continuously finds itself reacting to crisis, where the members of the school feel victimized, and where leaders who take charge, unfortunately, revictimized the people in the school? The case study may be an example of this. In the end, schools similar to the one in the case study lack one major ingredient when crisis occurs. They lack the leadership that can help schools become resilient to any new crisis. The idea that schools can avoid crisis in the twenty-first century seems outdated and insufficient. If leaders in schools make a concerted effort to remain proactive, not reactive, then crisis intervention may lead to resiliency.

Effective Leadership

Effective school leadership may consider the phenomenon of crisis as an opportunity for resiliency. For example, in the case study, the successful victim/offender mediation helped heal not only the relationship between the two students but also sent a message that polarized faculty and students needed to heal. Also in the case study, by a letter of reprimand to the school principal, the superintendent made a statement that the administration is fair, and there was enforcement regarding boundaries of acceptable behavior. Both of these decisions helped uphold the climate of the school and made it more resilient to future crisis. These decisions marked a proactive, not reactive, response to crisis.

Finally, it becomes important to identify what is gained by establishing resiliency in the climate of a school. Resiliency in schools helps to form long-lasting relationships. In the case study, the superintendent's decision demonstrated compassion and social conscience in considering the emotions of people in the school. Resiliency in schools helps to reinforce a sense of critical thinking where school members can be responsible for their actions. In the case study, the victim/offender mediation sent a message that personal responsibility is an unspoken rule upheld in the school.

Resiliency in schools helps in promoting creativity. In the case study, the superintendent could have let the legal system dictate the outcome of the crisis. However, the superintendent went beyond the principal's decision of upholding order and took a more democratic approach to the problem, thus demonstrating creativity along with social responsibility. Resiliency in schools helps set the tone of optimism. In the case study, the school climate became more resilient when the superintendent created a sense of optimism where solutions were possible and had a purpose, and that reward and punishment were not the only options available in school conflicts.

SCHOOL VIOLENCE AND CRISIS

It seems the connection between violence and crisis intervention has received media attention through numerous school shootings, weapons found in schools, and even cyberviolence (Shariff 2009). At this point, it may be important to list other possible violent situations that require crisis intervention. Harassment (as in the case study), physical threats, menacing behavior, disturbing the peace (noise), criminal mischief and trespass, all may be preludes to violent acts, both at the scholastic and the collegiate levels (Blanchfield, Blanchfield, and Ladd 2008). Such acts are usually associated with law enforcement where students, parents, staff, and strangers may be charged with a crime, and many learning institutions rely on law enforcement to protect school safety.

For example, the U.S. Department of Education created the Campus Security Act of 1990 to address violence both at college and public school levels. Emergency Management for Higher Education (EMHE) and Ready and Emergency Management for Schools (REMS) are guidelines that address procedures for effective crisis intervention in schools from the U.S. Department of Education's perspective. Some of the elements in these documents include preestablishing roles for faculty, staff, students, and first responders; conducting drills and exercises with faculty, staff, students, and community partners; and purchasing equipment and technology necessary to improve campus safety and preparedness (U.S. Department of Education 2011).

It may be important for school leaders to realize that other methods of violence prevention are as necessary as emergency interventions when violent acts occur. In the case study, one form of violence prevention strategies used by the superintendent was victim/offender mediation between the two students. Many schools and college settings have long established school mediation and peer mediation programs (Cohen 1999). Other violence prevention programs include forms of restorative justice programs such as school mediation or peacemaking circles. Such programs have become alternatives to strict law enforcement practices when incidences such as harassment, physical threat, disturbing the peace, and other precursors to possible violence are present in schools.

SUMMARY

This chapter points out the benefit of school leaders having an awareness of the people, places, and things that may lead to violence, and other forms of crisis. Awareness of troubled youth in the Columbine massacre, or unusual behavior as reported in the Virginia Tech shootings, are examples. In such cases, the main concern was the physical safety of those experiencing the crisis. Yet it was also pointed out that after "being safe" that "feeling safe" may be a leader's responsibility in maintaining the climate in a school.

In response to people in the school climate feeling safe, leaders may need awareness of those early warning signals or triggers that become signs of potential violence or crisis. Recent crises happening in public schools or major universities, for example, the Penn State sexual scandal (Rubikham 2012), could have turned out differently if school leaders understood the ramifications of ignoring these warning signals.

Effective school leadership needs a crisis intervention plan for dealing with potential crisis, and the trauma created by the crisis. It may be when the crisis has passed that leadership meets it biggest challenge. Is the crisis going to make the school more vulnerable to future crises, or will the school develop resiliency with reoccurring future crises? The saying "With change comes opportunity" is relevant for today's twenty-first-century school leaders.

The idea of crisis avoidance until a crisis is present seems naively reactive, rather than proactive in an environment where trauma and violence are possible. A fundamental plan of action needs to be in place with the hope that it is seldom used. When the people in schools know such a plan exists, and can be implemented effectively, the perception of "feeling safe" may be as important before and after a crisis happens as being safe becomes important during a crisis.

Chapter Three

Trauma

To a certain extent, this chapter is an extension of the discussion held in chapter 1, with similar themes. However, it is important to look at school climate not only from a crisis intervention perspective, but also from the perspective of trauma. Crisis intervention and trauma are intricately connected, and it is hard to talk about one without reference to the other. Crisis intervention reflects specific procedures, while trauma is the background in which these procedures gain relevance. Furthermore, trauma usually is left to the expertise of professionals like psychologists, psychiatrists, and mental health counselors.

Yet in the twenty-first century, it is hard to imagine effective leaders at the scholastic or the collegial level of education not being involved in under-

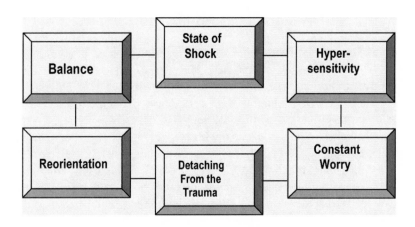

Figure 3.1. An Outline for Trauma

standing the impact of trauma on schools (Haravuori et al. 2011). One only has to be aware of media coverage of violent actions happening in schools through school shootings, tragic accidents, and shocking suicides, to realize that effective leadership may be more than having an understanding for school programs, or controlling the variables of budgets, curriculum, and staffing of personnel. In the twenty-first century, effective leadership in schools also carries the responsibility of knowing and understanding the impact of school-related trauma.

In this chapter, we present democratic leadership and its response to school-related trauma. It may be important to point out that trauma is not only a biological and psychological phenomenon as found in such mental health disorders as Post-Traumatic Stress Disorder or Acute Stress Disorder (American Psychiatric Association 2000). Trauma can also have an impact on the physical, emotional, and psychological climate of a school. In other words, trauma is a phenomenon that can be experienced collectively, where the climate of the school may be influenced as much as trauma influencing individual members of a school.

Keeping this in mind, effective leadership in schools may require more than counselors, psychologists, or psychiatrists to give direction to a problem where people are experiencing trauma together. It raises the question, "Who is responsible for dealing with the collective trauma impacting the climate of schools?" Referring traumatized people to trauma experts during a school crisis is only part of the solution. Taking responsibility for the impact of trauma on the climate of the school becomes a challenge of leadership. It may be a combination of individual attention through trauma experts combined with effective leadership that defines effective resolution of trauma in twenty-first-century schools.

CASE STUDY

The car accident killed four students at Grimly High School. The community was waiting for a response from the school administration. Fortunately, at Grimly High School the leaders were aware of the impact such a trauma can have on the climate of a school. Normal procedures and activities were either put on hold or were adjusted in order for school members to cope with the tragic news. School leadership was not only concerned with the state of mind of those close to the students killed in the car accident, but they were also aware that the school had recently experienced the suicide death of one of the football players, and assumed the accident would rekindle thoughts and emotions of those close to that event. For a period of time, leaders of the school were focused on recognizing the shock their school was going through.

As it turned out, school leadership was correct in assuming the school would be in a state of shock. It was obvious that the climate of the school had taken on a different tone. Students and staff seemed overly sensitive regarding how people were talking to each other, and certain topics that pertained to accidents, death, and lost connections were constantly discussed, or were avoided at all costs. It was obvious that the climate in the school had become more somber and reserved, and that normal joking and other forms of humor now seemed inappropriate. It was as though the unspoken rules of the school climate had changed, and what was considered normal activity now was more serious and cautious.

Everyone seemed concerned about what would happen next. How would the school respond to the crisis, and what was the timeline for such a response? This reality was not missed by those in charge. Leadership was aware that school personnel and students would be expecting some response, and were also aware that without an effective response that anxiety, worry, and prolonged shock could severely influence the climate of the school. This was not a time for generalities. The school needed to make a specific statement to the concerns of its people.

The specific problem at hand was "How is the school going to professionally acknowledge the trauma while beginning a process of detaching from it?" Both were considered important, and an action plan needed to be in place that addressed these concerns. Fortunately, leadership had a detailed action plan for such tragic events. They had procedures for debriefings and information dissemination plans to help students and the community through this trauma. All of these procedures were aimed at helping the school detach from their hypersensitivity and shock. The leaders were aware that constant worry could, and possibly would, bog the school down in a climate of intractable trauma.

Slowly the climate of the school began to shift from trauma and tragedy to more normal behavior. What was most important about this slow shift toward normalcy was found in the assumptions of its leaders. They were cautious not to make unchecked assumptions about when the crisis was over. Over time, they looked for clues that indicated the trauma had normalized.

For example, were students and staff still talking about the accident? Had the families acknowledged appreciation for what had been done? Were activities beginning to look toward future projects that had little connection to the trauma? It was only when school leaders believed they had sufficiently answered all of these questions that a more normalized schedule of events took place. They had given the accident and the trauma it created the respect it deserved, and the school was ready to move on.

In the end, what was most important to school leadership was whether a sense of balance had returned to the school. Had the school climate been normalized? Was the experience of shock replaced with a sense of normalcy?

Had the school successfully made the transition back to normalcy by becoming more resilient, not more vulnerable? These were the questions in the minds of school leaders with policies that followed not as reaction plans to trauma, but proactive plans to make the school more resilient. These were the questions and actions that reflected true leadership during a traumatic period in a school's history.

TRAUMA AND SCHOOL CLIMATE

State of Shock

When a trauma hits a school, whether it is a violent act or the death of a popular student or teacher, the school will suffer from a state of shock at some level. Let us take a moment to describe what a state of shock entails. First, the people in the school will have some form of emotional reaction. To some, the trauma may feel threatening at many different levels. To others, the trauma may cause a disruption in how they function within the school. This is especially relevant if a similar incident occurs that reminds people of a previous trauma. Ironically, it does not have to be directly the same type of trauma, but similar.

For example, after the traumatic suicide death of a student, the school may have a similar reaction if, for example, someone gets hurt playing football. The school is still in a state of shock, and any vague reminder can set a recurring shock in motion. What this means for leaders in a school is the trauma remains an open memory for those in the school, and any directive to move on too quickly may retraumatize these people.

Schools need to heal as much as people need to heal, and when a school is in a state of shock school leaders need to realize that trauma upsets the school physically, emotionally, and psychologically. Leaders who move on too quickly may cause a series of mini-traumas, where leaders are criticized for a lack of compassion or some other form of insensitivity.

Effective Leadership

One might argue that in the case study, the seeds for future trauma could have been planted if school leaders had not recognized the serious impact the traffic accident was having on the school. As noted in the case study, effective leadership required an awareness of more than what procedures or policies needed to be in place during traumatic experiences. The leaders of the school were professionally aware of the impact shock can create in a school.

If we could use an analogy, "Sometimes being an effective leader is similar to being an effective nutritionist. For a nutritionist, not only must the food be nutritious, but it must also taste good." In the case study, both elements were present. The leaders were aware of the effects that shock can cause to the people in the school, but they were also aware of how to let school personnel know they had this awareness.

First, how many schools have procedures circling around budgets, curriculum, and state mandates, but have few doctrines that truly include the climate of the school when trauma disrupts this climate? Second, even with effective solutions for dealing with trauma, how many school leaders understand how to effectively communicate their concerns to people who are experiencing shock, physically, emotionally, and psychologically?

In the case study, school leaders did not inappropriately react to the car accident, but immediately formed a response that would minimize the impact of trauma on the school. The leaders understood trauma and the shock it created in people. From this understanding, they formed strategies that included the human ramifications that shock placed on school personnel, in conjunction with instituting procedures dealing with school trauma.

Hypersensitivity

This leads to another common characteristic of school-related trauma. Usually, there is a sense of hypersensitivity or oversensitivity to many of the issues developing in the school during this time. It may be important for leaders to look for those sensitive triggers that develop with staff and students. Sometimes marking places where symbols of respect or mourning can be expressed to counteract this hypersensitivity can help normalize a school climate. For example, if students are killed in a car accident, it can be expected that friends and acquaintances may be sensitive and need to express their feelings through some gesture or ritual.

We all have seen flowers and symbols at the side of the road that mark the memory of someone killed in a car accident. Such rituals help mourners normalize their hypersensitivity to their grief by giving them an outlet for their emotions. Schools also may need to consider normalizing hypersensitivity through counseling when trauma strikes. Having counselors available or having specific rituals performed are gestures to help normalize the hypersensitivity caused by trauma. Effective leaders need time to normalize hypersensitivity and focus on making the proper gestures to relieve the trauma affecting the school.

Effective Leadership

In this particular case study we were faced with two phenomena that seemed to hold similar importance to the leadership role in the school. The first was the idea that hypersensitivity in schools was a real phenomenon. In the case study, the death of four students in the car accident may have created a hypersensitive reaction in other students, where the car accident serves as a reminder of their personal problems. This can create a series of mini-traumas, vaguely related to the original trauma.

Probably the example that has gotten the most attention is "copycat" suicides after the suicide death of an individual student. The other point of view pertains to what is an effective post-trauma protocol that may include counseling services, debriefing procedures for other students, acknowledgment through rituals, meetings, and other forms that recognize the loss of community members.

In the case study, it was important to recognize the car accident increased the hypersensitivity in the school, where other problems not connected to the immediate trauma could have surfaced unexpectedly. Expanding services to include help for other problems beyond the present traumatic incident seems a more comprehensive solution to these problems. In the case study, the leaders of the school did not neglect the issue of hypersensitivity and worked from a position that other traumas not related to the car accident may surface.

Constant Worry

When a trauma strikes, it is not only shock and hypersensitivity that are felt among the people in the school. There is also the possibility for constant worry taking over the thoughts of those participating in the school, whether it is teachers, administrators, or students. Here is an emotional experience that needs clarification for effective school leaders. There is a difference between worry and concern, and effective school leaders may need to understand this difference. When people in a school are "concerned" about a trauma, they tend to be specific and operational in their thinking. However, when people in the school "worry," they tend to overgeneralize their thinking.

The free-floating worry experienced by people in schools who are experiencing trauma may require school leaders to be specific about the *what, when,* and *where* services are being offered. In other words, it is the responsibility of leadership to change worry to concern for those in the school. For example, if someone brings a gun to school and the police respond by confiscating it, that does not mean participants in the school have stopped worrying about the trauma of having a gun in school. It may require words from school leaders stating the school's concern about school safety, even when the threat has passed. Keeping people informed about the state of trauma may be as important as the trauma itself.

Effective Leadership

The issue of safety has become a major theme in the field of leadership both in public and private schools and in colleges and universities (Jimerson et al.

2006). It would be hard to imagine effective leaders in both scholastic and collegial institutions not being aware of the importance of safety issues. When experiencing trauma, safety concerns can be expressed through the constant worry of the people in schools. In the case study, what was effective came through the actions of school leaders, who went beyond a reaction to the car accident. Initially, school leaders did announce to students and staff that an incident had taken place.

Yet effective leadership when experiencing trauma may require more than information dissemination. It may require changing peoples' worry to concern. Having concerns about a traumatic incident, as in the case study, is normal. It is when those concerns turn into constant worry that trauma tends to increase. In the case study, school leaders did not miss the potential for reducing trauma by only focusing on information sharing.

Effective leaders help change people's worry to concern by listening to their trauma, and by giving as specific information as possible and constantly updating those in the school when new information is available. Schools need to be specific and operational about dealing with school-related trauma, and changing one's worry to concern can reduce trauma in schools.

Detachment from the Trauma

In helping people detach from a major trauma that shocks a school, school leaders may need to possess a level of personal resilience in order to model how to let go of trauma. The idea that time will eventually bring the climate of a school back to normal may be too risky a proposition. It requires leaders to help others in detaching from the trauma, and letting the trauma go. This is not always easy for those most affected by school trauma.

However, at some point, schools need closure on the trauma, and without closure portions of the trauma may hang in the air for many years. For example, the Columbine High School shootings are still hanging in the air regarding tragedy in schools (Gimpel 2012). The leaders in schools may have the responsibility in helping those traumatized in the schools to detach and move on.

The first step may be to convince the people in schools of the importance of detachment. In order to detach, it may be necessary for school leaders to recognize what has been lost. That is why having an assembly or using a newsletter or some other form of communication may be necessary to let people know what happened during the traumatic experience.

The second step is for leaders to openly supply services where people in schools can deal with their personal trauma and where they can help others work through the emotions connected to the immediate trauma. Any time one experiences trauma, one also can experience a sense of loss. Again, using the Columbine High School shootings, it was important for people in the school to grieve the loss connected to their collective trauma, and also to find a way to detach from it.

Effective Leadership

In the case study, the leaders of the school understood the importance of detachment from trauma. This may require leaders to understand how people actually detach from traumatic events. The common myth is that, at some point, people in trauma start a new beginning. However, in effective leadership, you may consider that you need to end something first before a new beginning can be effective. Ironically, effective transitions *begin with an ending*, which is usually followed by some form of confusion until a new beginning is possible. In other words, people need time to readjust when people are traumatized, where something has to end before something new is possible.

Effective leadership when experiencing trauma may consider finding closure to the traumatic event prior to initiation of drastically new changes in schools. In the case study, there was a consensus among school leaders that normal school policies and procedures would not be initiated until the students and staff had moved on from talking about the accident, the families had acknowledged what had been done, and staff and students seemed anxious to move on. It appeared the school had a plan to effectively detach from the trauma.

Reorientation

Trauma in schools may go through periods of shock, hypersensitivity, worry, and detachment, but at some point it requires school leaders to create a new path after the trauma is over. This leads to some form of reorientation that gives new direction to the school and its members. Obviously, such an endeavor takes time and should not be rushed or forced on those in the school. However, at some point, changing traumatized schools to something new may be the responsibility of the leaders in these schools.

This stage seems to be least understood by those in charge of school administration. In many ways, with crisis comes opportunity. When schools are disrupted by trauma, it also becomes a period when new policies and behaviors are more amenable to change. (Let there be a note of caution in this section. This is not implying that after a trauma that impulsive and reactionary methods should be introduced, such as changing an entire set of school policies based on a single incident.)

Historically, we have seen such reactionary behavior in the creation of zero tolerance policies in numerous areas that may include driving, dress codes, and cell phone use, or in the establishment of certain school policies such as locker searches, searches with drug dogs, and overreactions through blending education with law enforcement. This is not to say that such policies are unnecessary, but correct timing becomes an integral ingredient in effective leadership. More important, during a time of trauma in a school, reconciliation may outweigh reactionary policies, where people come together not in fear but in solidarity, and where those in charge eventually form policies that deal with the problem instead of coming up with solutions that are a reaction to the problem.

Balance

There are important questions to consider when trying to reorient schools following a severe trauma, namely, "Is the reorientation to normalcy going to leave schools more vulnerable, or is it going to make schools more resilient?" This may first be answered by considering the belief systems of its leaders. If school leaders assume that trauma in school is inherently bad, then avoidance of trauma may be more significant than working through it. In reality, defining trauma in terms of it either being good or bad misses the nature of trauma. Trauma is a conflict that exists in a world filled with uncontrollable variables. How one approaches trauma may be an ingredient for defining effective leadership.

In the case study, the leaders of the school approached the car accident in the same manner as the incidents reminding school members of their personal traumas. They worked from the assumption that "trauma is trauma" regardless of its source, and changed the focus from "How do we survive this immediate trauma?" to "How does this trauma make the school more resilient to trauma, in general?" Like any social system, whether it is a family system or a school system, eventually systems will find a way to get back in balance.

It may be the responsibility of school leaders to make sure the balance includes growth and change in the school instead of lost freedoms and effectiveness. For example, after a student was brutally beaten by another student, the school cracked down on all students by restricting free time, separating students in the lunchroom, and followed this by giving strict detention for anyone being seen in the hallways without a pass. Here is a policy based on the school experiencing the shock of a brutal beating that was highly sensitive to students and staff and caused increased worry only to be resolved by aggressive policies that caused more shock and more worry.

Another way to approach this example would be in finding balance by acknowledging the brutal beating and the possible bullying experience going with it. A leader could take action on peoples' hypersensitivity and form a group to develop a plan that minimizes such traumas. The leader could also be effective by detaching this incident from punishment, and instead reorient the problem by setting up a bullying program to educate staff and students about violence in schools. The first plan reacted to a traumatic event. The second responded to the event by seeking out a reorientation plan that kept balance within the school.

Effective Leadership

In the case study, we experienced leaders who knew what was important in restoring balance to the climate of the school. Beyond the issue of safety, school leaders' main concern during trauma may be to restore balance to the school climate. This requires leaders to understand some of the workings of a school system. For example, any system, whether it is a biological, electrical, or in the case study, a school system, will seek out and eventually find some form of homeostasis or balance.

However, this does not necessarily imply the balance that is found is functional. We only have to turn to families where some form of addiction prevails, where other nonaddicted family members will enable the addicted member to keep the family in balance—unhealthy, yet in balance. In the case study, leaders were aware of returning the school back to a sense of normalcy, but not only in order to await the next trauma to unfold. The trauma was considered an opportunity to put the school back in balance—a balance that was resilient to future traumas.

SCHOOL VIOLENCE AND TRAUMA

Trauma has the potential for creating numerous forms of violence whether physical, psychological, emotional, or cultural (Underwood 2011). When people in schools are in trauma, numerous unspoken rules of behavior may change. For example, physically, people may be more on edge and be overly cautious about sharing information that before the trauma was automatically shared. As stated previously in the chapter, people may be oversensitive or hypersensitive about information shared that is personal or related to other traumatic events.

Culturally, people experiencing trauma may be less open to cultural differences and find themselves moving toward culturally familiar groups of people. All of these phenomena indicate that trauma can have a polarizing effect on the people in the school and can lead to some form of potential violence. However, the opposite is also correct. Shared trauma can unify a group into common purposes and convictions. For example, on September 11, 2001, the destruction of the World Trade Center had unifying characteristics connected to it, where strangers came together to help each other (Greenberg 2003).

Therefore, the connection between violence and trauma, in certain school-related experiences, may be controlled by the actions of its leaders. In the case study, we see the actions of school leaders diminishing the possibility for violence by having a strategic understanding of traumatic shock, hypersensitivity, constant worry, an understanding of the importance of detachment, effective plans for reorientation of staff and students, and finally, an understanding of when the school was back in balance.

The leaders in this case study diminished the chances of violence that counteracted the trauma by setting up guidelines that encouraged resilience in the school. There is no such experience during traumatic changes in schools without the potential for conflict, inasmuch as there are no traumatic changes being made in any arena without the potential for conflict, where violence is one form of conflict.

It may be that proactive leadership in trauma-filled schools reduces the potential for violence. Through understanding the shock behind traumatic events, school leaders can respond directly to the shock instead of just reacting to it. By understanding the hypersensitivity to those in trauma, school leaders can neutralize highly explosive triggers that lead to violence.

Furthermore, by addressing the concerns of school personnel during trauma, school leaders divert the anxiety and tension that accompanies constant worry, where constant worry may lead to direct or indirect forms of violence. Historically, violence and trauma seem to have strong connections with explosive outcomes (Schwab 2010). Yet leaders managing trauma in schools do not necessarily lead to forms of violence. Such trauma may have the opposite effect by unifying and making more resilient those who have learned from the traumatic event.

SUMMARY

Though leaders in schools are not necessarily trauma experts, the responsibility for the effects of trauma on the climate of a school becomes a paramount concern any time violence, crisis, or unexpected emotional disruptions change the tone of those within schools. Schools can be in a state of shock much like the people in them. Recognizing the effects of shock on a school and having an emotional response that is appropriate and effective are necessary ingredients in treating trauma in schools.

For example, it may be important to acknowledge that people in schools can become hypersensitive when going through trauma, and that school leaders may need to adjust their thinking and responding through recognition of this hypersensitivity. It also may be important to recognize that a school where people are constantly worrying causes more anxiety, and that changing people's worry to concern gives them a specific plan for coping with trauma.

In spite of successfully dealing with trauma, schools are primarily institutions where learning and socializing take place. The ability to successfully detach from trauma allows a school's purpose to continue. Somewhere in the post-trauma experience can be a window of opportunity where people in schools begin expecting a sense of normalcy to return. Returning too early may cause increased trauma, while returning too late may bog down a school for many weeks, months, and in some cases years.

This makes having a plan for getting back to work extremely important, where one considers the emotional trauma present in the climate of the school, while at the same time, moving on in a more balanced and resilient capacity. Unfortunately, the experience of trauma can be viewed as the hidden curriculum in some schools. Having an effective response to trauma now seems a mandatory inclusion into the role of being effective leaders in schools.

Chapter Four

Emotions

Peoples' emotions in a school setting may be a part of a hidden curriculum of feelings, communication patterns, and attitudes understood by more democratic school leaders. This is in contrast to more traditional methods of school leadership, where responsibilities lean more toward supervisory tasks and duties. This chapter assumes that being aware of the emotions found in the climate of a school can have an impact on the role of school leadership, and that others in the school influence a leader's effectiveness based on what they believe, how they feel, and how they behave toward each other.

In other words, school leadership carries the responsibility for decisions on procedural issues, even though the school's emotional climate may dra-

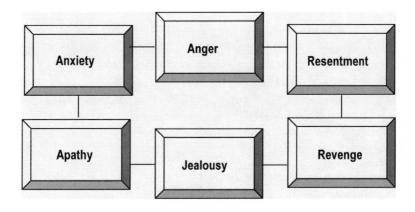

Figure 4.1.   An Outline for Emotions

matically effect these decisions. For example, budget cuts causing resentment may have a different outcome if people in the school feel empowered.

By understanding the basic emotions that cause conflict or violence in schools, educational leaders can set the emotional tone for more positive responses to school conflicts. Six emotions that historically have caused conflict and violence in schools will be reviewed: anger, resentment, revenge, jealousy, apathy, and anxiety. The intent is to bring an awareness of how emotions have an impact on the climate of a school. Leadership in schools has an opportunity to take a more democratic approach regarding emotions and the tasks required to supervise and manage a school (Hoffman, Hutchinson, and Reiss 2009).

Management and supervision do not happen in a vacuum. They take place in a climate filled with emotions that can have an impact on their success or failure. Such awareness requires more than human relationship training. It requires an understanding of emotions from a more democratic perspective.

Counselors, school psychologists, and other helping professionals have historically covered the role of emotions in schools (Reback 2010), yet the responsibility for emotions affecting the climate of a school falls under the responsibility of school leaders. This becomes even more important when the school is experiencing violence or other forms of crisis.

When a school is in crisis, who will be the person or persons who recognize the emotions surrounding those in crisis, and who is responsible for doing something about it? The following is an exploration of those emotions that may affect school leadership, and what may be appropriate responses to these emotions. When considering emotions affecting the climate of a school, a more democratic vision of leadership may be necessary.

CASE STUDY

Scenario 1

It seemed the humanistic philosophy that had gained the education department high praise at a prestigious liberal arts university was now in disarray. There were threats from the administration that jobs would be cut, and the graduate school of education seemed a likely candidate for cutting, from what was a predominately undergraduate institution. The philosophy of university leadership was to "cut off the limbs to save the tree," though the limbs being cut were the healthy ones.

The chairperson of the department made the decision to cut popular courses, discussed the demise of the department if things did not change, and made arbitrary decisions without informing department members. The emotional climate had shifted from an empowered group of staff and students to a climate of resentment, where doors were closed and conversations were discussed among a select few. The department was in conflict, and the chairperson indiscriminately wanted to discuss changes in procedures that would satisfy the university's administration regarding cost cutting. The chairperson was determined to effectively "prune the tree."

Such an approach caused anger and resentment that soon led to moments of jealousy, greed, and hatred among those in the emotional climate of the graduate school. People were angry for not being informed with little discussion or input. They found the immediate ultimatums unreasonable. However, the department chairperson seemed to be practicing tunnel vision, and plowed ahead regardless of the concerns from others. Unfortunately, this action became oppressive and drove the faculty and staff members into their offices where they talked about the chairperson's insensitivity, their panic, and not much else.

Some of the faculty and staff decided to get revenge by not offering their services when it was needed in the department. Others became defensive of the "turf" they had secured over the years, and defended it by making sure untenured and more vulnerable faculty became the victims of future budget cuts. In the end, the students and faculty commented on how much they hated being in the graduate school building, and how rejected and alienated they felt from the rest of the university.

Scenario 2

The graduate school of education became aware of the upcoming budget cuts, and realized the emphasis would be on keeping undergraduate programs at a predominately undergraduate liberal arts university. Though the philosophy of the university was to "cut off the limbs to save the tree," the chairperson of the department called special meetings of faculty and staff to develop ways that helped the university, but also enhanced the effectiveness of the department. The first meeting was solely for invited members to vent their anger, even though it was obvious to everyone involved that things had to change.

Those involved took the liberty and vented until the chairperson posed the question, "What can we do better while bringing in more revenue for the university at large?" Common ground and agreement from both long-standing department members and untenured, less-experienced members, along with input from graduate students, was reached that a better and more efficient department was the goal. There was also agreement reached that long-standing rituals and department positions may have to change in order to maintain a vibrant working relationship with the rest of the university.

Meetings were called, and the chairperson assigned specific topics to selected groups of people. One group had the responsibility of making the department better without losing its humanistic philosophy. Another group was responsible for creating new markets, while another group explored the possibility of creating new programs. Even though the climate of the department demonstrated high anxiety, it was doing something about it. The department was taking a stand, and regardless of the outcome, people were going to stand together. In the end, the faculty and staff presented a proposal to the administration.

First, they stated that the department's history of offering a humanistic view of education based on a liberal arts background needed to be marketed through university admissions as a selling point. Second, that graduate programs could be revised with the addition of "bridge courses" so that undergraduates could stay a fifth year, thus creating a new source of revenue for the university. Third, a campaign to establish common ground between the graduate and undergraduate faculty would be implemented. This initial plan did not guarantee that cuts would not be made to the graduate school of education, but it did improve the emotional climate based on a sense of pride in the department by showing creativity and flexibility to the rest of the campus.

EMOTIONS AND SCHOOL CLIMATE

Anger

Expressions of anger in schools can be confusing. First, any sign of anger can be viewed by school leadership as a warning signal for controlling future conflict. Ultimately, if anger explodes in schools, the responsibility falls on its leaders to contain it. However, school leaders may expand their perception of anger in schools, and view it more comprehensively. Take, for example, a student getting angry in a classroom setting, or a freshman exploding with anger in a college dormitory. From a personal healing perspective, the venting of anger may be a step needed to relieve frustration, as opposed to keeping it buried and accumulating over time.

This is understandable when realizing that many of the violent acts witnessed over the past few years in schools were the result of buried anger, rather than chronic anger (Feindler and Engel 2011). However, the venting of anger is a different goal than school leaders trying to control angry outbursts in schools or universities. For effective leadership, anger often needs a level of regulation in order not to breach the rules and guidelines of the school.

The venting of anger in schools usually can be addressed by a practicing counselor or mediator, where anger is expressed as a safety valve so future explosions do not take place. By recognizing the importance of occasionally venting anger in schools, it may be in the leader's best interest to understand anger that cannot be tolerated, as opposed to expressions of anger that have a purpose and reason attached to them. Indiscriminate anger that disrupts the school's mission and the school's rules becomes the responsibility of the school leader in upholding the guidelines of the school.

As for anger that has purpose and meaning, leaders may give a response that focuses on solving the problem connected to the anger. For example, anger expressed by disputants in a school mediation program may be important in upholding one of the tenets of democracy, if dealt with in a civilized and professional manner (Reidel and Salinas 2011). Furthermore, leaders who avoid anger at all costs may create a larger problem for either response to anger, whether maintaining the guidelines of the school, or helping someone solve a problem. Trying to avoid or burying anger may quiet the explosion, but it may make things worse in the future.

Effective Leadership

In the case study, the chairperson in Scenario 2 understood that faculty/staff and students had a meaning and purpose behind their anger, and called a meeting that included the venting of emotions as one of its purposes. The chairperson went beyond the role of administrator and became a conciliator and mediator for the department. The case study is an example of a common set of circumstances in today's sparse economy, where anger can be viewed as a natural response to budget cuts, lost salaries, and layoffs.

As the case study indicated, the department was faced with a conflict that required problem-solving skills along with effective emotional management of school personnel. Conversely, in Scenario 1, the chairperson reacted to potential economic cutbacks by initiating procedures that were viewed as unreasonable by faculty and staff. It was the chairperson who fueled anger in the school. In Scenario 2, the chairperson recognized the potential for anger, and proactively created a forum for expressing it. Here we see an example of a chairperson who knew the difference between anger that had a purpose and meaning and indiscriminant anger.

Resentment

Resentment appears to be more acceptable in a school setting than expressions of anger. Some people refer to resentment as buried anger, but that only begins to capture the essence of resentment in schools. Resentment begins with people feeling frustrated and stuck with the circumstances presented to them when in conflict. With resentment, people will bury their frustration, and it remains as buried anger until a moment arises, where subtle and indirect expressions of it become possible (Ladd 2005). That is why leaders who chronically suppress anger in schools may fail to notice the resentment that has spread just under the surface of the climate in schools.

For example, a school filled with resentment may explode when a simple disagreement allows for an explosion, where all those buried frustrations are allowed to surface in the form of gossip, innuendo, and sarcasm. School leaders who can skillfully deal with anger when it presents itself can avoid the buried anger and frustration found in resentment. For emotionally empathic, democratic school leaders, it may be important to realize that resentment can be one of the major causes of lateral violence such as gossiping, bullying, cyberbullying, or activities that bog down the school functioning correctly and efficiently. Although resentment appears as more civilized than anger, it can be an emotionally damaging problem in schools (Ladd and Churchill 2012).

Effective Leadership

The case study in Scenario 1 reflected a common outcome of ineffectively dealing with resentment. When people find circumstances unreasonable, but do not have the ability to express themselves, they can implode while accumulating resentment and feelings of powerlessness. This leads to another important point when resentment has filled the emotional climate of a school. Effective school leaders may need an understanding of the difference between a predicament and a problem, when conflict faces the school community.

In Scenario 1, the chairperson saw the mandate from the university administration as a predicament that needed to be followed. In Scenario 2, the chairperson saw the university mandate as a solvable problem. When feelings of resentment dominate the school culture, the ability of leaders to offer choices toward solving a problem helps people emotionally. In the case study, there was no guarantee that the university administration would accept the department's proposals, yet for the faculty and staff, being proactive and feeling empowered to make change may have warded off resentment and forms of lateral violence from taking place.

Revenge

Some people have misconceptions about revenge. It is believed that a person needs a formal plan in order to retaliate against others. In schools, no formal plan is needed for people to get back at each other. When someone feels violated, there is a natural tendency to get emotionally back in balance. Unfortunately, popular culture depicts this as "getting even," where people will bide their time until the violator is in a position for retaliation. This can be a problem for democratic leaders who recognize "bad blood" between one person and another, based on some form of violation. On occasions, schools have circumstances where camps are formed and where each party tries to get others on their side to justify their retaliatory plans.

One of the bigger problems revenge causes in schools is the loss of common ground needed to emotionally keep people together. In a subtle, yet significant, way the loss of common ground in schools, where people feel polarized into groups, can be the breeding ground for revenge, even though nothing yet has happened to warrant a reaction to vengeful behavior. We can see this happening in such circumstances as on August 17, 2012, when a Baltimore teenager felt polarized from the rest of the student body and wanted to get back at the school by opening fire on them—fortunately only one person was hurt (Lynch 2012). The important point to remember for school leaders is that no formal plan is needed in order to seek revenge. All that is needed is for someone to violate someone else.

Effective Leadership

Revenge seems to have an escalating effect on the emotional climate found in schools. For example, in the case study in Scenario 1 most of the department felt violated by the actions of the chairperson. This created an escalating effect where older faculty members looked for ways to violate younger, untenured faculty. Again, as stated above, no specific or formal plan existed for such actions to take place. Without proper leadership, violations can lead to retaliations, and retaliations can turn into new forms of violations.

In Scenario 2, the chairperson was aware of the escalating problem in the department. People felt violated, but instead of taking it out on each other, the chairperson formed a plan of solidarity where the department would propose a resolution to the university administration. People who feel violated have a natural tendency for getting emotionally back in balance. Plans that help accomplish such a goal are based more on justice than revenge (Ladd 2009). The case study in Scenario 2 was about "what was our plan?" Was it about taking out the threat of cost cutting on each other, or was it about developing a proactive plan to resolve the matter for the department?

Jealousy

Schools are places where socializing constantly takes place, and people experience the fear of losing—control, power, time, face, and many other fears of something being lost. For example, the leadership in a school may discipline two disruptive male students wanting to be with the same female student, based on the jealous reactions between them. Or, school leaders may have to confront professional jealousy of faculty and staff when the conflict of ownership and "turf" become problematic. Jealous of people's time, turf, influence, control, or power are all issues that may warrant a sense of jealousy in schools. Jealousy is about being afraid of losing something and putting in a claim to keep it.

As stated previously with resentment in schools, leaders are in a position to help with jealous issues by finding common ground among jealous individuals or groups. With enough common ground, there may be no reason for jealousy. For example, many forms of violent acts have their roots in jealousy, such as domestic violence (Buzwa, Buzwa and Stark 2011). However, if there is substantial common ground developed between jealous people, it has the impact of bringing people together, rather than separating them through jealous claims for something they are afraid of losing.

Furthermore, jealousy can cause problems in schools because it can justify the use of force. Jealous people can feel justified in using force based on the assumption "they are getting back something that was theirs in the first place." However, schools are about learning, and ownership of learning in schools does not make sense.

Effective Leadership

One observes the seeds of professional jealousy being planted in Scenario1, in the case study. The chairperson created a climate where the older faculty members became afraid of losing something, and put in their claim for preferable treatment, if budget cuts came to pass. In Scenario 2, we see a different outcome. The chairperson created common ground between the faculty and staff so claiming and counter claiming was not a part of their behavior. At this point, it may be important to note that jealousy can eliminate much of the trust that is found in a healthy climate between cooperating individuals. In other words, jealousy runs the risk of eliminating trust that is needed in facing conflicts, and in solving problems.

In difficult times, as found in Scenario 1, jealousy can disrupt an organization by destroying the trust to effectively solve problems. The loss of trust in leaders to lead, or the loss of trust in the organization itself, becomes an emotional issue that has a dramatic impact on an organization in initiating effective problem solving. Jealousy can polarize groups of people as much as trust can create common ground among them. In the case study, the emotional climate may hold equal importance in solving issues surrounding budget cuts, yet in Scenario 1, the leader of the education department failed to see that connection.

Apathy

Apathy is generated by experiencing too much trauma, and schools are not immune from the phenomenon of apathy. Many people in education and other institutions refer to this experience as "burnout," and some suggest that we live in an age of apathy (Dilulio 2006). Let us make an analogy to explain apathy. If trauma was water in a glass, then apathy happens when the glass is full. In schools where unresolved trauma is prevalent, apathy accumulates in the school and eventually can create an atmosphere where people believe they have lost their meaning and purpose.

This can be summed up in the statement "Who cares?" The effect apathy has on school leadership can be profound, especially for those leaders who have created a positive climate for their institution and have motivated their people to believe in it.

In a school experiencing apathy, people may find themselves numb to the problems of the school, and decide not to become emotionally involved in the school's climate. One of the most devastating facets of apathy in schools is when people lose respect and hope for conditions improving the climate of a school. There can be a slow deterioration in the school climate when unresolved crisis becomes the focal point in people's thinking. For example, apathy can be the end result of angry people eventually becoming resentful, and resentful people eventually experiencing apathy (Ladd 2007).

Effective Leadership

The case study in Scenario 1, the chairperson's decisions not to communicate with the faculty, to make arbitrary decisions without consulting others, and to threaten gloom and doom for the department may have added more trauma to an already apathy-prone situation. The chairperson was going in the opposite direction, and disregarded the importance of people feeling hopeful when facing trauma and solving emotionally charged problems.

In Scenario 2, the chairperson called a meeting to listen, not to judge. Faculty and staff were given an opportunity to vent their anger and resentment connected to the problem, and they were given hope by creating an action plan for dealing with the problem. This example makes reference to the democratic nature of effective leadership in schools.

Giving hope to people in crisis can have the opposite result than letting trauma fill people with apathetic feelings. Hope can re-establish meaning that may have been lost through the experience of apathy. In Scenario 2, it was only after allowing for an expression of feelings that the chairperson became more directive and procedural. It was going to take a motivated staff to solve the problems of the department, a staff that could envision some form of hope for the future. School leadership may want to consider the emotional climate in a school and the impact that apathy has on it and the sense of hopelessness that can develop any time trauma becomes a part of the equation.

Anxiety

Leadership in schools may need to look more carefully at some peoples' notion that all anxiety is detrimental to the functioning of an institution (Martinez-Monteagudo et al. 2001). A school needs a moderate amount of anxiety to function. Anxiety helps people focus on problems, and it is only when people continuously cannot solve their problems that the detrimental aspects of anxiety take over. In mental health, anxiety disorders are not caused by people having anxiety, but by not being able to stop having it (Ladd and Churchill 2012).

For leaders in schools, moderate anxiety may be defined as "excitement" or "positive tension" that can be used to motivate others. There may be value found in school leaders monitoring the level of anxiety in schools, rather than trying to avoid it. Leadership that practices an avoidance of problems or focuses only on part of a problem may be creating increased anxiety in the school climate.

Effective Leadership

The two scenarios in the case study demonstrated two approaches for resolving anxiety. Scenario 1 overlooked the anxiety experienced by the faculty and staff, while Scenario 2 made an effort to directly deal with people's anxiety. The chairperson in Scenario 2 understood that the faculty and staff needed specific information in order to face the anxiety connected to potential budget cuts. The chairperson gave them as much information as possible, but also helped them take a stand and develop a proactive plan. It may be the ability to take a stand on anxiety that helps in reducing it.

Democratic school leadership may want to consider the difference between anxiety and fear when caught in anxious situations. Anxiety is based on uncertainty; however, fear is the ability to recognize a threat and take a stand in dealing with that threat. Unforeseen events, such as budget cuts, can throw a school into a climate of anxiety, where leadership may require having others take a stand, in spite of the personal fear connected to having to take such a stand. The chairperson in Scenario 2 may eventually have to face cuts in faculty and staff, but without taking a stand and facing the problem directly, the outcome has a different effect on the emotions of people in the department.

SCHOOL VIOLENCE AND EMOTIONS

At first glance, it may appear that the issue of violence in the case study is not necessarily relevant. We are talking about university professors and staff. How violent can they become? For the most part, people experiencing budget cuts do not necessarily become physically violent. Yet it may be this case study that helps us expand one's definition of violence facing leaders in schools. Beyond forms of physical violence are emotional and psychological violence, and these characteristics are relevant to the case study. This also raises the issue of school leaders practicing violence prevention as well as violence intervention.

For example, bullying in schools may begin initially with psychological and emotional violence that escalates into physical violence. Let us not rule out the potential for emotional and psychological violence causing deterioration of an effective set of guidelines and norms found in schools. Through anger, resentment, jealousy, revenge, and apathy, schools can become surprisingly violent places. Violence comes in many forms, and the emotions found in this chapter generate their own forms of violence. Only associating violence with the emotion of anger may be too narrow a connection for violence affecting the climate of a school.

For example, beyond anger is resentment, and it dictates its own form of violence. In today's schools, the issue of lateral violence through gossiping, cyberbullying, favoring only the high achievers, and other indirect methods may create a subtle, yet psychological and emotional, atmosphere for future violence. Resentment becomes the emotion of choice in civilized and bureaucratic institutions where anger is not tolerated.

In a school setting, indirect lashing out found in resentful behavior relieves people's frustration about school problems, but without actually solving them. Take for example resentment in some teachers' rooms in public schools where character assassination can be viewed as a way of relieving stress and anxiety, while concurrently being viewed as a psychological and emotional form of violence.

Psychological and emotional violence may also be linked to jealousy, where "professional jealousy" can influence the climate of a school. Turf battles over curriculum, promotion, and teaching methods can negatively have an impact on the school's mission and practices. Outside of schools, jealousy can be the major cause of violence, such as in domestic violence, that can find its way into schools (Blanchfield, Blanchfield, and Ladd 2008). School leaders should not rule out the loss of motivation or a sense of outrage created by these disputes, or the apathy and revenge experienced when left unresolved.

Violence and emotions cannot be separated regardless of the subtleties connected to certain emotions. An understanding of the impact emotions have on schools may be the first preventive step to warding off physical violence in schools. Schools and their leaders are vulnerable to many forms of violence from outside influences, where little control is possible in stopping these occurrences. That does not mean that leadership cannot control the emotional climate of a school by understanding the dynamics involved when violence from outside school borders has an impact on the emotions of people residing within its borders.

SUMMARY

We have seen in this chapter that the emotional climate of schools may be different than the emotions found in each person. The emotional climate is the collective feeling that people in schools have about what is happening at any given moment in the life of these schools. There are times when the emotional climate is filled with hope, and people in schools are excited and motivated to do well. Other times, the emotional climate experiences conflict where emotions like anger, resentment, revenge, jealousy, apathy, or anxiety fill the air with a certain tone that affects the emotions of others at any given moment.

In this chapter, we are making a statement that effective school leadership goes beyond following rules, guidelines, or procedures or other supervisory duties. More democratic school leaders may need an understanding of the emotions in which many of the guidelines or procedures are being acted out. It may be the collaborative combination of guidelines and procedures along with awareness of how people are feeling about school that balances out effective leadership in schools.

Furthermore, an understanding of those emotions found in conflict situations in schools such as anger, resentment, revenge, jealousy, and others may create a foundation for conflict prevention as much as intervention when emotional problems dominate the climate of schools. In some respects, the emotions in schools are the "elephant in the room" of effective school leadership, where a peripheral understanding of them may not be enough. This is not to suggest that school leaders are replacements for school counselors, psychologists, school mediators, or outside helping professionals.

What it means is that one of the responsibilities of effective school leadership may be to take into account the emotional climate of the school, while leaving individual emotions to other helping professionals. Effective school leadership is made up of several important ingredients such as being constructive; building for effective outcomes; being an effective coach, teacher, and mediator; and making sure supervision and organization are reasonable and productive (Lukaszewski 2008). Adding to this list is leadership that takes responsibility for the emotional climate of schools, where an awareness of emotions and how they affect schools acts as the background where other leadership activities take place.

Part II

Prevention

Chapter Five

Empowerment

Empowerment, a term that has many popular connotations in education, psychology, sociology, and other disciplines, is when people gain control over their lives as the end result of an experience (Zahrani 2012). It becomes a process that generates a sense of power in individuals for use in important matters that affect their self-esteem. However, the idea of power in the context of empowerment does not exist on its own. It can be found in relationships between people and things.

In the field of education, empowerment is not viewed as giving people power, but in providing opportunities, resources, and support so that they can empower themselves (Azaiza 2011). Empowerment is a process that allows students, faculty, and other staff members to take action and make decisions

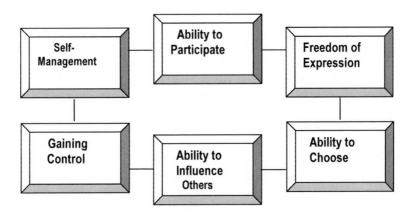

Figure 5.1. An Outline for Empowerment

in autonomous ways, where people feel a sense of control over their future in the school.

The following chapter takes into account the value in empowering people in schools. It demonstrates that people can be valued members of a school community, regardless of their social status or their cultural heritage. It describes how a school leader can encourage frustrated school members to participate in the spirit of the school by fostering freedom of expression, allowing the ability to make choices, and showing how disenfranchised students can influence others. Furthermore, it discusses how empowerment is the process of gaining control over one's self with the eventual goal of having a sense of empowerment through self-management.

Some researchers have stated that schools are one of the least democratic institutions, where empowerment becomes problematic for teachers, students, and administrators (Farenga 2011). Others make the statement that leaders in schools have a social responsibility to create a climate of democracy, where empowerment becomes one facet of this democratic process (Gale 2011).

A democratic school leader may consider empowerment in schools beyond being only a part of the school's mission statement. Empowerment may be a practical element in maintaining a safe and violence-free school, where oppression, loss of freedom, or stagnation may inhibit learning while increasing the chances for direct or indirect forms of violence.

Empowerment becomes the opposite of oppression. When people in schools feel the freedom associated with a sense of empowerment, school conflict becomes more tolerable. It softens the blow when crisis enters a school. It helps the people in schools become resilient when disruptions or conflicts threaten the school climate.

CASE STUDY

Donna, the newly hired principal of James Middle School, was determined to make a difference in her new role. As a woman of color, she had experienced both racial and economic prejudice in her advancement to her current position. Yet Donna took democracy in school seriously and viewed it as a practical matter rather than as a platitude found in the school's mission statement. Specifically, her major concern was in finding ways that all students in the middle school felt empowered to learn and have a sense of human development.

Within a short period of time, it became clear to Donna those areas where oppression of learning were subtly being practiced, even though the objectives of the school dictated a more humanistic and democratic story. The most blatant example of "talking the talk but not walking the walk" was in the middle school's resource room, where the judgments of other students, staff, and administrators acted in subtle yet condescending ways toward these students. This problem was exacerbated by the fact that many of the resource room students were of color and came from low socioeconomic backgrounds.

Through Donna's inquiries, she found that this was not the only problem facing resource room students. They also accepted the subtle prejudice found in the sentiments of other students and professionals, and guardedly, yet jokingly, referred to themselves as "retards." They became the focal point of numerous jokes, even though other school members made sure the joking was politically correct. Donna believed they were receiving proper services from the resource room staff and faculty, but she also believed that an elusive prejudice about these students had infiltrated the school climate and was setting the tone for other indirect forms of prejudice to be viewed as acceptable, though hidden and hardly ever discussed.

As the leader of the middle school, she found the curriculum and other school-related policies adequate; however, her assessment regarding the climate of the school was that it was unacceptable. She made the decision to empower the resource room students in order to bring equality and democracy to the climate of the school. She believed that if people in the school felt some form of empowerment, the climate of the school would shift from what she presently perceived as empowerment for a select few to empowerment for all. Her first step was to interview the resource room students and determine how they could contribute to the climate of the school.

For example, she discovered that many of these students had difficulty with writing, yet they excelled in drawing. Under the guidance of the resource room teachers, these students began to plan and execute the making of murals on a portion of hallway that was scheduled for repainting by the building and grounds staff. She allowed the students to choose the themes for the murals, with acceptance of these themes subject to approval by Donna. When all of the murals were completed, Donna invited the media, parents, and other community members to judge their favorites and to plan for future murals to replace the present murals. She also allowed input from the judges in determining future themes for the murals.

Over time, Donna noticed a significant change in the climate of the school. The prejudiced joking about resource room students had stopped. More important, what stopped were the disparaging labels that resource room students gave to themselves. Resource room students had a meaning and purpose in the school they could own with pride. They were empowered and had gained a sense of control over their place within the climate of the school.

In the end, they also learned self-management skills that had a significant impact on their self-resiliency, and they were better able to cope effectively with their individual disabilities. Donna had directly empowered these students to be a part of the school, while indirectly fighting dynamics of prejudice and oppression. The school climate had changed significantly, no matter how subtle or insignificant it appeared to others before her empowerment project took place.

EMPOWERMENT AND SCHOOL CLIMATE

Ability to Participate

Before feeling empowered, people need a chance to participate in schools. School leaders who believe in the principles of democracy accept the importance of empowerment by letting others know the value associated with some form of collaborative school participation (Friend and Cook 2009). This may be a fundamental ground rule for anyone who wants to create empowerment in schools. However, it is not the type of rule that can be understood without school involvement.

It may require the leader to announce and make clear that participation is welcomed. One of the mistakes that school leaders can make is to tell people they can participate, only for them to discover later that they cannot. As stated in the case study, this can be viewed in schools as "talking the talk but not walking the walk." Telling people they can participate, but not letting that happen, can create a climate of resentment, leading to an increased sense of oppression and possible violence.

Effective Leadership

Here are several effective leadership skills that encourage participation and set the stage for a climate of empowerment in schools. First, it may be necessary to share goals and direction with those within the school. In the case study, Donna made a point to meet with resource room students and staff and determine the most effective venue for including these students within the climate of the school. She did not simply share her sentiments about including these students. She helped them develop a formal plan filled with direction and goals. Second, she approached inclusion of these students as a problem to be solved, not as a forum for pinpointing problem people. Her mission was not to place blame but to work together in improving the school's climate.

Finally, she listened first before providing guidance. In the case study, Donna talked to students and staff to determine the proper method for empowerment. She did not enter the resource room with a plan for "what should be accomplished" according to her personal expertise. Her expertise in empowerment was to listen and ask questions. This helped empower the resource room students and staff by recognizing their ability to participate.

Freedom of Expression

Empowerment is not something that anyone can see. It is an experience where a person feels they can express themselves, where what they say means something. When people in schools have lost their freedom to express themselves, resentment may replace freedom in the school climate. A democratic school leader allows students, staff, and parents the freedom of expression, even at the risk of disagreement.

In more democratic schools, being empowered to make a statement or advocate for a belief connects empowerment with freedom, even when people agree to disagree. Effectively establishing empowerment requires more democratic school leaders to consider a problem-solving method of leadership as much as methods for upholding the school rules.

Sometimes, school leaders uphold the rules without allowing for any freedom of expression, whether it be in the school, classroom, or community. In a school that advocates for democracy and diversity, people unable to express themselves can limit the usefulness of empowerment efforts in schools. Even though freedom of expression may cause conflict, it also creates a platform for diversity and democracy. There is a difference between conflicts based on problem solving and those based on conflicts that break the rules of a school. Understanding this difference lies at the heart of a school leader's vision of empowerment in schools.

Effective Leadership

In the case study, Donna empowered those in the school that were unable to stand up for themselves. A combination of their learning disabilities, combined with the negative perceptions of others, restricted their freedom of expression. They knew and accepted the disparaging remarks made about them but lacked the freedom to express their unique perceptions of being in school. Donna provided them with the freedom of expression based on their artistic strengths. She gave them a voice in the school and empowered them to express that voice.

It may be in highly competitive, achievement-oriented schools where the voice of nonachievers is curtailed. This is not based on having little to say, but instead on the loss of power they experience when they are unable to achieve as well as others. Democratic leaders who believe in empowerment demonstrate the value they place in all members of a school. This is indicative of the behavior demonstrated in the case study, where Donna invested her efforts in giving a voice to students with learning disabilities.

It seems that some school leaders struggle with giving a voice to under-achievers, and this struggle may be found in their confusions over their beliefs. There may be school leaders who fundamentally agree with the tenets found in the case study in this chapter but may remark that "schools are about learning and achievement, leaving little time for such altruistic endeavors as empowerment." School leaders may consider which is more conducive to learning and achievement, and in the end, which constitutes a better school. Is it in an institution where freedom of expression is limited or in one where the freedom to express oneself is a common and acceptable part of the school climate?

Ability to Choose

There is no such thing as empowerment if people in the school climate lack the ability to make choices. It may be why more authoritative leadership styles based on directives or guidelines create compliance (usually through top-down methods) but do little in empowering people to feel a part of the school climate (Pepper and Thomas 2002). Lack of choices can create resentment, frustration, and dissention in schools, families, and workplaces.

Regarding empowerment, it is the ability to have choices, even when the choices are limited, that helps to empower members of a school. For example, many extracurricular programs in today's economy, such as sports and music programs, are considerations for the chopping block in local school budgets (Deford 2012). An uninformed leader may simply announce these cuts and run the risk of destroying the morale of the school.

Giving communities, parents, and students options and choices in solving problems does not necessarily end with finding the optimal answers. However, it can empower these people to be a part of the problem. Being a part of a problem creates a sense of ownership, even when the problem has little chance of resolution. School leaders may welcome empowering people when they can choose between two good choices, or they can act as advisors when explaining why one choice is better than another. In troubled times, it should not be overlooked that effective school leaders can still empower people by giving choices, even when the choices are negative.

Effective Leadership

In the case study, Donna initiated a subtle, yet important, unspoken rule that resonated through the entire school. She approached and engaged the most disenfranchised members of the school to participate in developing the climate of the school. She gave students with learning disabilities the ability to choose which artwork would be placed on certain walls in the school.

At face value, this may appear simply as a gesture of generosity. Yet Donna aimed beyond the resource room. She made a statement to the entire school and the community that choices were possible by using the art project as a model for a new attitude in the school. It was an attitude where people were empowered to make choices. Modeling choice making in schools allows for not only empowerment, but also for diversity in a school setting.

People from different cultural, ethnic, and economic backgrounds can make choices differently (Vyronides 2007). School leaders have a responsibility in helping students and staff in making correct choices. That does not mean students and staff need to make the same choices. In the case study, Donna knew the resource room students were less likely to choose being high achievers in the school.

A more democratic school setting may require a broader definition of achievement, where people are recognized for achievements of their own choosing. In the case study, Donna understood the importance of the learning-disabled students making choices that allowed for their style of achievement. She understood the connection between choice and empowerment.

Ability to Influence Others

An effective school leader who has created a climate where people feel they can participate, and where these people have the freedom to express themselves, along with the ability to make choices (even negative choices), are now in a position to influence others. Yet this reveals the controversial issue regarding the difference between empowerment and compliance. Sometimes, the concept of effective school leadership overlooks the difference between these terms, where compliance may marginalize empowerment, especially when one person feels they can influence another through acts of force (Hammonds 2012).

Leaders who force compliance through micromanagement or inflexible directives can lose an opportunity to influence others while denying others an opportunity to influence them. Overcompliance in a school may replace a sense of empowerment with feelings of resentment.

When school leaders empower others in schools, the statement being made is, "They have the power to influence you, and conversely, you have the power to influence them." It may be the reciprocal relationship between empowering leaders and empowered others that create a climate where people influence each other. Empowerment can be inhibited when people feel they have little influence.

Even in situations where the entire school is subjected to the control of outside forces, such as when there are state and federal budget cuts to educational programs, seeking out choices together will give others a sense of influence with each other, even when it is difficult to influence outside forces holding the ultimate power. Such influence may not change the outcome of decisions made from outsiders, but it may help maintain the emotional climate of the school.

Effective Leadership

In the case study, Donna allowed students with learning disabilities to influence other people's perceptions of them. She demonstrated their talents through art, but more important, she empowered them to become accepted members of the school community, members who established their unique ability to influence others. She created an experience where these students were accepted, recognized, and appreciated by others. It becomes acceptance not only defined as acceptance by others, but also in self-acceptance.

In the case study, Donna made these students recognizable through their art, and recognition was now possible. She fostered a deeper appreciation for those who live with disabilities, and she influenced others to also appreciate the experience of being a person with individual differences. All these characteristics gave these students influence while further strengthening empowerment in the school.

Gaining Control

Empowerment has a strong element where the center of freedom resides in each person. An ineffective school leader can wreck empowerment by limiting the freedom of people in the school. The irony of empowerment is when school leaders allow for freedom, for example, freedom of expression, freedom of choice, and so forth, leaders may also empower *their own freedom.* People in schools need a sense of freedom over their lives.

When a sense of freedom is outside the reach of the school community members, the guidelines and mandates from leaders may appear less tolerable or fair to students or school personnel. It is not that people in schools need to have complete freedom over their lives, but empowerment is possible when they have a sense of freedom over some portion of it.

Leaders have an opportunity to empower people by helping find their sense of freedom, no matter how insignificant that sense of freedom may appear. Democratic school leaders may consider a different set of skills beyond supervision and management. Today's schools may need leaders who understand a balance of power in schools, where top-down management may not be the most advantageous way to create freedom in schools (Bloom 2004). Effective school leadership may require empowering those in the school to discover their personal sense of freedom.

Effective Leadership

In the case study, Donna demonstrated how a leader in a school could help school members be empowered by allowing each person to find their sense of freedom. At the same time, she created an experience where her leadership enhanced control over issues such as prejudice and individual differences within the school's climate. This was in stark contrast to what was happening before she arrived. The center of control for the students with learning disabilities was found in the indirect and prejudiced remarks by others in the school. These people held the power over these students with disabilities to the point that the resource room students insulted themselves by calling themselves "retards."

Furthermore, effective school leadership may consider the effects of empowering school personnel with a sense of freedom, and its value in controlling one's mental and physical health. In the case study, the entire school seemed like a healthier place to work and learn after the empowerment of the resource room students. A school climate where people feel a sense of freedom becomes a place where anxiety and fear are less likely to influence teaching and learning.

Self-Management

One of the ultimate goals of leaders who believe in empowerment is for the school community to take responsibility for their actions and to practice some form of self-management. Self-management has the ingredients of the other steps to empowerment, namely the ability to participate, freedom of expression, ability to choose, influence over others, and a sense of control. When school personnel embrace such characteristics, they tend to rely more on themselves instead of constantly wanting direction from their leaders. This makes empowerment not only a way to create democracy, but also a method for being more orderly and efficient (Denison 2009).

The idea that leaders need to manage all aspects of the institution in order to maintain order and efficiency is an idea that disregards the value of empowerment. It appears to some outsiders, and to less informed leaders, that strong leadership is about taking charge and not appearing weak. The reality is that strong leaders become more powerful by allowing other people to develop a pattern of self-management. In this way, each person not only invests in the beliefs of the leader, but also invests in himself or herself.

Effective Leadership

In the case study, it appeared that one of Donna's goals was to direct James Middle School toward a position of self-management. By empowering those in the school who were least able to manage themselves, Donna set the tone for everyone else to value self-management. She skillfully created an experience where being responsible for your teaching and learning was considered as valuable as academic achievement. The case study in this chapter described the life of a real person and a real school event.

Though we have disguised the case study for anonymity, there are hundreds of examples in which a progressive leader believed in empowerment through self-management. For example, constructivist educational principles embrace such concepts as self-management and empowerment (Martin and Loomis 2006). Empowering the school community to manage itself can be viewed as a more democratic method of school leadership that does not abandon the traditional tasks of school leaders, but places these tasks in a climate where people feel empowered to manage themselves.

SCHOOL VIOLENCE AND EMPOWERMENT

The case study marks one example of the subtle, yet potent, outcomes of indirect violence in schools. It depicts students with learning disabilities and how they went from inflicting psychological violence on themselves to finding a sense of personal empowerment. This example is one of many where subtle, indirect forms of prejudice may be overlooked by school leaders until it manifests itself in stronger and more direct forms of physical violence.

When you take into account that the rate of learning disabilities among criminal offenders in the United States is 50 percent, and 31 percent of learning-disabled students are arrested three to five years after leaving high school (U.S. Department of Justice 2012), it brings into perspective the responsibility of school leaders to curtail more than blatant forms of physical violence.

However, students with learning disabilities are only one group of students that may suffer from the psychological violence through subtle forms of prejudice in schools. Racism, sexism, and homophobia round out prejudice and discrimination possibilities for school leaders. Leadership in schools should consider a more democratic view where the climate of the school receives equal attention as budgets and curriculum, and where an understanding of the value found in empowering people is given equal value.

However, beyond psychological violence in schools is the emotional violence manifested in such activities like name calling, humiliation, intimidation, and inappropriate kidding. This is the language of prejudice where the seeds of violence may form, and where empowerment can be lost in a climate of disrespect. When asked the question, "How do you get violence out of schools?" the first step may be by putting respect for each other back into schools. Empowerment is a concept that reinforces respect by recognizing, accepting, and appreciating differences, and empowering people who are different to make a significant contribution to the school.

SUMMARY

This chapter may indicate the difficulty in taking a concept like empowerment and making it an operational and practical part of a school leader's role in an educational institution. It appears that tangibles such as budgets, curriculum, and discipline codes are better suited for being organized, practiced, and assessed than the experience of empowerment. For those leaders who perceive themselves mainly as administrators, the experience of empowerment becomes even more problematic.

Concrete procedures in schools that can be visualized and utilized may be at the center of how one is defined as a school leader. Yet an experience such as empowerment, though hard to visualize, may have a larger impact on people than first imagined by school leaders. School violence is difficult to detect when it is forming in the climate of a school through resentment or frustration, however, empowerment counteracts violence in subtle yet substantial ways.

In this chapter, we took the elusive experience of empowerment and demonstrated it through the creativity of an exceptional middle school principal. Her success was found in her ability to take the experience of empowerment and turn it into a practical and operational part of the middle school. Leadership may be as inspirational as it is practical and concrete. Empowerment is one of those experiences that may actually improve concrete and practical aspects of school leadership. If the preceding statement is correct, it may call for a more multidimensional and democratic school leader to see the benefit in an experience that remains hidden to more management-oriented leaders.

In the case study, we saw the practices of one of those leaders. Her ultimate goal was self-management, a goal of many more traditional school leaders. However, her methods for creating this form of personal discipline banked more on using empowerment to accomplish her goal. Methods of linear thinking were replaced with more critical thinking, as she devised a way to improve the climate of her school. In doing so, she indirectly uprooted the potential for seeds of psychological and emotional violence.

As stated above, the experience of empowerment in schools may require school leaders to look at teaching and learning more multidimensionally. Today's schools put great emphasis on achievement through grades, athletics, and other competitive venues. Yet if modern school leaders decide to perceive their roles more democratically, then it requires perceiving students in the school from many different points of view. One of the subtle discriminations found in achievement-based schools is when scholastic achievement becomes the "Holy Grail" of what is valued in these schools, and where only high achievers are rewarded for being successful.

In a school that advocates for empowerment, achievement is still recognized, but so are honor and respect. Being rewarded and being honored are two different experiences. In schools, one is rewarded by following the rules that will obtain the reward. For example, if you get high grades you can go on the field trip.

In the case study, Donna did not intend to reward students with disabilities for their academic achievement. She wanted to honor them for their individual differences, and empower them to believe in themselves, regardless of their level of achievement. Only rewarding those who can achieve at high levels in schools can be viewed as a subtle form of prejudice. How many students with disabilities have not attended school trips, proms, or could not go out for sports because of their grades? Honoring students differs from rewarding them. Honor is based not on what students can achieve, but on who they are as human beings. Empowerment in schools is more about recognizing the humanity in people, regardless of their achievements.

This does not disregard the importance of achievement, but it balances being rewarded with being honored. Highly competitive schools may find themselves separating students into the "haves" and the "have-nots," where schools with an established climate of empowerment find common ground between students. Feeling empowered through recognition of one's individual differences is not perceived as a reward, but as an honor. In this light, empowerment becomes a form of achievement for those who have difficulty competing for academic rewards.

Chapter Six

Assertiveness

Assertiveness may be one of the fundamental communication skills needed in order to be an effective school leader. Assertiveness is primarily about advocating for yourself through clear expressions of your point of view. Yet assertiveness is more than clearly expressing yourself. It also includes respecting the rights of others and knowing that what is expressed will have an impact on them. In the climate of a school, assertive behavior can improve relations among students and staff by raising the level of self-esteem while they earn each other's respect.

Assertiveness can be a practical communication pattern in highly stressful schools where violence is possible and tensions run high. An interesting point to make is how assertive behavior can help stress management in

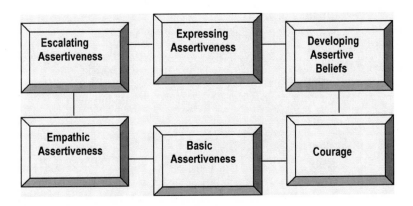

Figure 6.1.   An Outline for Assertiveness

schools, both as a prevention and intervention method of leadership (Morrison 2007).

However, having a clear understanding of self-expression in a school setting may be only half the equation for assertiveness in schools. Being assertive is not only about what you have to say but "how you say it" (Stewart and Lewis 1986). Assertive self-expression seems the optimal method school leaders have in getting messages across to others. For example, when school leaders deliver a message with little conviction or in a reactionary manner, their delivery may distort the message and lessen its effectiveness. In such cases, others may respond to the lack of conviction or reactionary delivery of the message, rather than the conveyed content.

This chapter will explore those factors that make assertiveness a contribution to the maintenance of a positive school climate. It will also address different levels of assertiveness, where an understanding of these levels may curtail the formation of violence both direct and indirect. However, it may be important to keep in mind that dysfunctional communication patterns are not unfamiliar to people in the climate of a school.

In some schools, much of the conflict experienced can be through using patterns of communication that do not work. Assertive communication may not be the norm of what people are used to, especially in conflict situations. It may require a school leader to establish a pattern of assertiveness and model it for others to follow in order to curtail potential conflict and violence.

CASE STUDY

Liberty High School was in a state of chaos. The former principal was considered a tyrant by both students and staff. Numerous threats and outbreaks of student fighting consumed the discussions throughout the school. It was so bad that the principal was eventually fired. The middle school principal was now in charge of finding some form of order in the school. George was a young, newly trained principal who showed great promise in his restructuring of the middle school, and the hope was that he could do the same for the high school. Unlike his predecessor, George did not attempt discipline techniques, which eventually led to law enforcement intervening when they did not work. George developed discipline around maintaining an effective but disciplined school climate.

For a number of weeks as the new high school principal, he listened and learned, attempting to identify the problems of the school. Based on his observations and much thought, he developed beliefs about the school that he shared with faculty and staff. He told them that in conflict situations it is not enough to tell students what to do. "We must also help them figure it out." He believed that many discipline problems were caused by classes that did not engage students, and he would be holding workshops on how to engage students more effectively. He said his goal was not in managing student behavior but in creating a climate in the school where they managed themselves. He said, "We cannot ignore the covert hostility of students by making them comply only with school rules."

We must do both: create structure and boundaries based on rules, but also respond to the emotions and behavior of students causing problems. He stated that his beliefs were not only based on the concept of "compliance with rules" but also in "maintaining a healthy school climate." After these statements, he opened the discussion and listened, while eventually finding consensus based on the requests of others.

For the next few months, George made a concerted effort to put his beliefs into practice. He realized that many of the conflicts created in the school were interpersonal problems between students or between members of the staff, such as relationship problems, peer pressure, personality conflicts, unhealthy competition, "turf" issues, and others. He decided to create a school mediation program that specifically dealt with problems based on opposing, yet legitimate, points of view. He believed in finding the correct solution to problems, and being proactive when problems came up. He understood that many interpersonal problems did not need a judge but rather a mediator, so people in dispute had an equal voice and an equal opportunity to express their points of view.

George's belief that many discipline problems emerged when students in the classroom were not sufficiently engaged led to the development of teaching skills workshops. More important, George developed a mentor program where master teachers with high success records mentored other teachers on different topics such as curriculum development, teaching styles, learning styles, and classroom delivery styles. He did this in a democratic way, where all teachers involved could be mentors in their specific area of expertise. No single group of master teachers mentored all other teachers.

George believed it was a mistake to completely control his teachers, and giving up small amounts of control for mentoring purposes would empower his faculty to help each other. What he did not do is mandate a school-wide program of discipline, but let teachers work together on a discipline policy that matched their needs. He approved policies as long as the policies created structure and boundaries, and that student emotions were not left out of the equation.

With change comes conflict, and this was no different at Liberty High School. The following months were filled with tense moments as George's policies took hold in the school. He had long discussions with passive teachers who were close to retirement and wanted to ride out the last few years of their career by changing as little as possible. He offered these teachers scheduling changes that avoided chaotic classes before or after lunch. He met with what some faculty called the "town bullies," euphemistically referring to those aggressive teachers who seemed to create more problems than resolutions.

He made a series of statements, from asking them to change their style of discipline to eventually letting them know the consequences if they did not. He joined discussions in the "Teacher's Room," where helpful and constructive discussions about students had a tendency to turn ugly. Teachers outside the Teacher's Room advocated for students, but in the Teacher's Room they ridiculed them, and made belittling comments about certain students and their families. George let them know the importance of healthy venting, and how emotionally draining the experience of teaching can be, yet he also created ground rules about no name calling, gossiping, or judging of students and their families.

George's main goal was to change the tone and tempo of the chaos in Liberty High School. His focus was not to change one set of rules regarding discipline with another stronger set of rules. His goal was to create a more assertive and functional school climate where aggressive, passive, and passive-aggressive forms of interaction were replaced with assertive methods to improve the school. George did not give structure to the school, but restructured it in a more democratic and assertive manner, where people were responsible for their actions. He created specific methods of conflict resolution that matched the types of conflict found in the high school. This was not a "one discipline policy fits all" method, but a proactive, assertive attempt to replace chaos with democracy.

ASSERTIVENESS AND SCHOOL CLIMATE

Expressing Assertiveness

Schools can become positive places of expression when leaders establish assertiveness within these schools. The subtle, yet important, ability to express oneself effectively sometimes slips under the radar of criteria for managing schools. In an age of increased violence in schools, assertiveness becomes the art of self-expression that may define an effective leadership style. Keeping this in mind, it may be important for any school leader to ask this question, "Do I know the difference between aggressive, passive, passive-aggressive, and assertive behavior?" In order to establish assertiveness, clarification of these terms may be the first step.

The term getting the most attention in schools today may be the definition behind aggressiveness. Aggression is based on standing up for your point of view in ways that violate others, and this includes the actions of aggressive school leaders. Blaming, punishing, and violating other people's rights add to an aggressive leadership style that can destroy the climate of a school. Leaders who demonstrate aggressive communication can be the leading contributors in establishing resentment in schools.

Such aggression can send communication underground, where school personnel complain about the school leader and his or her aggressive leadership style. Furthermore, leadership aggression can cause subtle forms of revenge, where premeditated plans are drawn up to get back at school leaders (McAdams and Foster 2008).

In comparison, the other side of being aggressive may be the damage created by a passive leader. It appears that a passive leader may cause revenge, where very little gets addressed or resolved in the school. This is where people seeking revenge ignore the rules of the school and develop their own rules, knowing their passive leaders will not stop them. Finally, there is the hybrid "passive-aggressive leader" who acts passively, yet is aggressive behind the backs of those in the school, generating both resentment and revenge.

Being assertive is standing up for yourself in ways that *do not* violate others. Expressing oneself effectively in schools may require a clear understanding of the difference between assertiveness and other more dysfunctional forms of self-expression.

Effective Leadership

In the case study, George understood the different styles of self-expression found in Liberty High School. He understood the dysfunctional communication styles that were now dominating the climate of the school. He realized that such forms of self-expression were reactionary attempts to deal with the chaos found in the school. He also knew the school had not clearly identified their problems but were prematurely reacting to them.

School leaders may need to understand how people in schools are ineffectively responding to each other. Also connected to how people are responding is the issue regarding what types of conflict are causing these responses. It becomes difficult for school leaders to assertively respond unless they understand different types of school conflicts (Blanchfield 1983).

In the case study, George understood that making judgments based on interpersonal conflicts between two opposing points of view was a losing proposition. He established a school mediation program so both points of view were heard. He also knew that classroom management was best handled by students attending interesting classes. He used the school's resource of effective teachers to mentor those having difficulty in the classroom. He realized that being assertive with unhappy teachers required negotiation that showed these teachers an appreciation for their points of view. Although, in the end, he knew this required their commitment to the school.

Developing Assertive Beliefs

Our beliefs lead to our behavior, and this is clearly demonstrated in a leader's beliefs about self-expression. One of the first problems facing leaders with potential violence brewing in schools becomes their lack of clarity about how to express themselves to others in conflict. They may express themselves through habit: "It worked for me at my last employment. It should work for me now."; or they may have learned to express themselves from their family of origin: "It worked for my father. It should work for me now."; or from past experiences: "I always meet aggression with force."

Such inherited or evolved beliefs seem too vague for demonstrating an effective style of self-expression in schools. In order to be assertive in schools, it may require leaders to adopt a few generalized beliefs that fit most conflict situations (Siddiqui 2011). Here are a few:

- A belief in respecting one's self and others
- A belief that it is important to express oneself clearly
- A belief in expressing one's honest and appropriate feelings, opinions, and needs
- A belief that it is better to be proactive than reactive
- A belief that conflict inherently is neither good nor bad. It depends on the circumstances.

Much of the lateral violence found in schools, such as gossiping, name calling, negative sarcasm, and so on, are based on an opposite belief system than the above five beliefs. Lateral violence feeds on disrespect for others, not respect. It is usually hidden in some confusing message, and may not be an expression of one's true feelings. Lateral violence is a negative reaction to another person or group. It has few proactive characteristics. It works from the belief that violating others is a justified form of conflict resolution.

Effective Leadership

In the case study, George understood his beliefs about conflict and leadership. He decided that a "one-size-fits-all" form of conflict resolution did not address the school's different conflict problems. He believed that problems with differing points of view needed mediation, and problems that required direction needed mentors. He realized that constantly focusing on students for discipline problems was not the entire problem. It left out the boredom created by uninteresting classrooms. He directly dealt with retirees and aggressive teachers by negotiation and by clearly explaining consequences.

All of these assertive procedures were based on his belief system. In other words, his beliefs led to his behavior. How many times have ineffective leaders overreacted to a conflict situation instead of acting through their beliefs? Assertiveness can be less effective without beliefs backing up one's assertive behavior. Furthermore, school leaders who have clear beliefs can model them for others to follow. Having others know a leader's belief system creates a sense of consistency, rather than one where anxiety is connected with leaders who constantly change their minds.

Courage

Effective school leaders can demonstrate a level of courage about their beliefs when dealing with school climates that have turned toxic and dysfunctional. An aggressive school climate can become bigger than the assertive communication of its leader. Schools where the aggressive behavior of students is only matched by the faculty and staff may require the courage of its leaders to restore a positive school climate. Courage is not as problematic when the climate of a school is clear, respectful, and appropriate. However, what action do leaders take when it is not? In these cases, courage may require *working through* conflict, rather than *reacting to* it (Rustin and Armstrong 2012).

The irony is that people in conflict may have less difficulty understanding an aggressive leader than an assertive one. Assertively changing a school filled with conflict may take an act of courage. It may take courage to go against a school climate, where others have established dysfunctional patterns of communication that are diametrically opposed to the beliefs of assertive leaders (Treasurer 2011). How many leaders fall into the trap of reacting to conflict by becoming aggressive, or how many leaders react to conflict by becoming passive, or possibly passive/aggressive? Leadership when expressing assertive behavior may require an act of courage to work through a negative school climate, rather than reacting to it.

Effective Leadership

"Commitment is healthiest when it's not without doubt, but in spite of doubt" (May 1994, 37). This could have been the sentiment of George, the principal of Liberty High School, when he decided to change the school's chaotic climate into a stable place for teaching and learning. It was less risky for George to match the chaos in the school with some form of ultimatum. This seems the method of choice among those school leaders who want a quick solution for reducing crisis or conflict (Evenson et al. 2009).

However, he did not believe in such ultimatums, such as those found in "zero tolerance policies." He believed these policies escalated conflict rather than reducing it. Instead, George listened to the concerns of the high school personnel until he identified specific, workable problems. Then he tried matching a conflict resolution method that fit each problem.

To some leaders, upholding rules is less risky than solving problems, especially if leaders cannot solve those problems. George demonstrated the courage of his beliefs and addressed the school in an assertive and proactive manner. In a chaotic school climate, being assertive may become the strongest form of self-expression. Chaos breeds aggressive, passive, and passive-aggressive forms of expression.

Courage seems a necessary ingredient in assertive behavior along with clarity of one's beliefs. George demonstrated a clear understanding of the problem to the high school faculty and staff. Yet it still took courage to work through each problem with them; he did not know completely whether what he proposed would work. In spite of this, he did not overreact, but instead faced the school's conflicts head on. He assertively committed himself to his beliefs with the hope that his beliefs were correct.

Basic Assertiveness

Let us now turn our attention to different types of assertiveness in schools. *Basic assertiveness* is a straightforward expression of beliefs, feelings, and opinions. For example, a school leader might say, "I want this type of cooperation among faculty members," or "I feel that it is a mistake to use this form of discipline in the classroom." In both of these examples, the leader lets others know exactly where he or she stands on these issues. In order to be effective, basic assertiveness may require a review of some communication skills that are indicative of assertive behavior (Hoffmann 2009).

First, what is trying to be expressed may require a leader to be the focal point. Here are two examples of being the focal point: "These are the procedures *I want you to follow* on the class trip," or "*I am upset* about how the class trip was handled." In both of these examples, the leader has the courage to take responsibility for what was needed and what was felt. This is basic assertiveness, as opposed to "Try not to get in any trouble on the class trip," or "Let us consider a new format for the class trip next year." Such mystifying statements may seem subtle and harmless, yet they create an opportunity for confusion and conflict in schools.

Effective Leadership

In the case study, George made himself the focal point for change. Instead of blaming the faculty and staff for problems in the school, or judging the current climate in the school as unacceptable, George clearly and directly pointed out problems that he had observed and proposed solutions to problem areas that he would like to try. His assertiveness was in making himself the focal point. For example, he stated that he observed these problems, and it was he who wanted to change them.

However, he kept himself open for changes in the plan and sought out a sense of consensus. It became his assertive attempt to identify the problems as *he saw them*, and *he stated them clearly to others*, which defined his basic assertiveness style. He demonstrated a style that others in the school recognized as different from the chaos previously experienced from the former authoritarian school principal at Liberty High School.

Empathic Assertiveness

Some people in a climate of assertiveness believe that a leader's assertive expressions are only about the leader, and in some cases this may be true. However, a leader can also be effective by having an empathic understanding of another's point of view. *Empathic assertiveness* works well when another's point of view needs to be respected and heard by the leader (Wildman and Clementz 1986). Sometimes basic assertiveness is all that is needed to resolve conflict in a school.

However, empathically considering another's point of view allows leaders to be accepting of others while still being assertive. For example, leaders who say, "I understand the time and effort put into creating that elective course for students and *I believe it is an important course*, but for now I need to put it on hold until we straighten out our budget problems."

It is possible to be assertive and recognize legitimate yet opposing points of view. During the course of any school day, there are conflicts that may arise where leaders make assertive judgments, yet still recognize the legitimacy of differing viewpoints. Actually, being assertive in disputes where differing points of view are legitimate, but not acknowledging these differing viewpoints, may be interpreted as ineffective leadership.

Leaders can be assertive and still respect differing points of view (Holt and Marques 2012). Some leaders forget they can be right and wrong at the same time. Their behavior can be appropriate and correct, but not considering the points of view of others makes their behavior appear inappropriate or aggressive. In certain situations, it is appropriate to agree to disagree with other points of view.

Effective Leadership

It must be noted in the case study that George not only demonstrated basic assertiveness skills but also empathic assertiveness. He realized that the presentation of his plans for change to the faculty and staff could cause opposition, so he opened the discussion so others could be assertive while he listened to their concerns. This form of empathic assertiveness where a leader listens then allows others to also be assertive is common among mediators and negotiators who want to minimize aggressive and passive-aggressive forms of self-expression.

The ability to be assertive combined with the courage to receive assertiveness from others may be at the root of conversations surrounding democracy in schools. Basic assertiveness is the ability to make your message known in a clear and proactive manner. Empathic assertiveness is the ability to listen to others and let them know their feelings were heard.

Escalating Assertiveness

Leaders in schools have the same rights as any other person in the school. However, what happens when someone in the school fails to respond to the leader's basic assertions and continues to violate the leader's rights? Sometimes, one fails to realize how being an assertive leader has an impact on the structure and boundaries of a school climate. For example, aggression in schools has a tendency to break down rules and boundaries governing the school as it might in destructive, gang-related violence. Passive or passive/ aggressive behavior has similar effects on school boundaries and rules, such as when there is gossiping and destructive communication from peer groups.

Assertive behavior may be the most effective method leaders can turn to when upholding the boundaries and rules of a school. Think for a moment about schools where the aggressive behavior of the school leader was partially responsible for violence erupting in a school. Leaders that use escalating assertiveness may make sense in a climate of a school, when the boundaries or rules are in jeopardy. More than any other person, school leaders are responsible for upholding the boundaries and rules of an institution.

So, what is *escalating assertiveness*? It is when other assertive styles of communication have failed and a leader needs to uphold the boundaries and rules of the school. For example, a teacher in a public school continues to preach their religious beliefs, even though the school leader assertively tells the teacher to stop preaching religion. An assertive leader may first express basic assertiveness by stating, "I want you to stop teaching religion in your classroom." If the teacher continues, the assertive leader may express empathic assertiveness by saying, "I respect your religious beliefs and understand how strongly you believe in them, but I need you to stop teaching them in the classroom."

Finally, if the teacher continues to violate the wishes of the assertive leader, he or she may say, "If you do not stop teaching religion in the classroom, I will be forced to bring this up with the school board because it is against the law." Escalating assertiveness is what the word implies. It is an attempt at assertiveness when all other attempts have failed to make a difference. For the most part, people in the climate of a school have a higher probability of accepting and perceiving as fair an escalating style of assertiveness, when other styles have failed to produce results (Dallas 2011).

Effective Leadership

The case study pointed out numerous examples of escalating assertiveness. George's encounters with retirees, bullies, and Teacher's Room gossips were all examples of having to attach consequences to one's assertiveness. In the end, most assertive leaders would rather influence others without consequences being connected to the assertions. Assertiveness thrives when leaders do not have to remind or threaten others with consequences. Sometimes emphasizing the consequences turns the intent of one's assertions toward being perceived as threats.

In the case study, George went out of his way not to threaten the retirees, bullies, and teachers in the Teacher's Room. He wanted there to be change by pointing out consequences, not dwelling on threats. This subtle, yet overlooked, difference may separate escalating assertiveness from threats or insinuations. There is no reason to threaten or to force one's consequences on others when escalating assertive communication is handled correctly.

SCHOOL VIOLENCE AND ASSERTIVENESS

Most forms of violence in schools begin with small exchanges between people, where gossiping or blaming sets the stage for other forms of violent expression. Keeping this in mind, an open commitment to being assertive by school leaders can be combined with each leader's personal style of communication. When leaders say nothing during conflict situations, anxiety can fill the school, and when leaders overreact, they may create hostility in schools. In the case study, it was not only the steps that George took to change the climate of the school, it also was his assertive approach to sharing these steps with others. It can be a dangerous, unchecked assumption to not consider the impact of a school leader's voice, language, intensity, and emotional delivery when trying to make changes to the climate of a school. Furthermore, remaining silent during times of conflict may send the message that one may be complicit with the conflict situation, as can be understood through recent scandals such as what took place at Penn State in 2011 (Johnson 2012).

For school leaders, there also may be certain ways of self-expression that appear to others as the "language of violence." A review of these styles may help in differentiating assertiveness from other forms of self-expression in schools. For example, defamation is a false accusation of a person's words or actions that harms their reputation (Roberts 2011). In the case study, George was concerned about the discussions in the Teacher's Room for exactly this reason. He assertively tried to end possible violence through the expressions of defamation of character.

Another example was his assertiveness regarding teachers who were labeled "town bullies." George understood the danger of words that created a sense of verbal abuse. He understood the danger in harassing, interrogating, accusing, blaming, insulting, lying, berating, taunting, putting down, discounting, threatening, name calling, yelling, and raging at others (Brennan 2003). All of these forms of self-expression create the potential for violence in schools. Aggressive communication can encourage forms of abuse, while being assertive limits the potential for abuse (King 2004).

School leaders may need an expanded definition of violence in schools, beyond physical violence. Self-expression can lead to emotional, cultural, and psychological violence as well. For example, the "language of violence" in schools may lead to emotional violence, where people feel frustrated and stuck with what was said and to consider retaliation for these verbal violations.

Or, the "language of violence" may cause cultural violence by polarizing people into gangs where they feel safe in justifying violence toward others. Finally, the "language of violence" can set the tone for underlying anxiety that psychologically eats away at the infrastructure of the school's climate, where caution, stress, and trauma replace safety, trust, and compassion.

SUMMARY

Communication is a major part of being a leader in a school environment. The self-expression of school leaders sets the quality and tone for how others express themselves. School climate can shift significantly if the quality and tone of its leaders becomes too aggressive, causing others to experience feelings of oppression. Conversely, leadership that communicates a passive indifference can leave the school climate open for a loss of direction and possible chaos. School leaders combat oppression in schools with the fairness conveyed in being assertive, while concurrently creating reasonable boundaries that combat loss of direction and indifference.

This chapter gives numerous examples of the importance found in assertive self-expression. For example, George combated oppression in Liberty High School by finding conflict resolution strategies such as the school-wide mediation program. He also created boundaries that combated loss of direction and indifference by assertively confronting "town bullies" and by negotiating for the support of soon-to-be retirees. In these examples, George set the quality and tone for communications in the school. He demonstrated leadership through assertive self-expression.

However, being assertive through self-expression may not be enough. Effective school leaders may need to know why they are assertive, and they need to have a formalized belief system that is clear to themselves and others. Effective school leaders should demonstrate the purpose behind their assertive behavior. This requires the courage of knowing and practicing one's convictions and beliefs, even in circumstances filled with conflict. In conflict situations, assertiveness can become the less-used form of communication, where aggressive communication is more common and understood.

In the case study, George showed the courage of his convictions and presented his philosophy of leadership through his actions when facing conflict at Liberty High School. He also realized that different forms of assertiveness were needed to face these conflicts.

This chapter reveals that another form of assertiveness is empathic assertiveness. It combines empathy with a willingness to have others answer to a leader's responses with their own form of assertiveness. Again, in the case study, George negotiated with faculty close to retirement and helped them become a part of the changes in the school. This demonstrates that an effective leader can listen to others and still practice assertiveness.

In spite of basic assertiveness or empathic assertiveness, school leaders are faced with circumstances that require an escalation of assertive self-expression. Consequences may be required when the statements of a leader are not followed correctly, or when others fail to comply. This is where the art of assertiveness becomes crucial. The ability to make people accountable while remaining nonthreatening is the line that separates assertive from aggressive leadership.

This also can be the line that separates violent from nonviolent forms of self-expression in the climate of a school. Unfortunately, self-expression can become a secondary concern to some school leaders who overvalue administrative procedures while undervaluing how their administrative directives are being received by others. Subtle forms of violence in schools may be generated by how information is received in the school, rather than by how the content is conveyed.

Chapter Seven

Common Ground

One of the best definitions of *common ground* comes from the *McMillan Dictionary*: "Common ground is something that people can agree about, especially when they disagree about other things" (McMillan 2012). Common ground may be one of the most important conflict resolution skills available to school leaders when problems permeate a school climate. Yet how well is common ground understood and utilized when these problems enter a school?

Historically, school leaders solve such problems by first focusing on the disagreements and differences between those in conflict (Sleegers et al. 2009). This is understandable based on the logic behind analyzing differences between people and then finding solutions to resolve those differences.

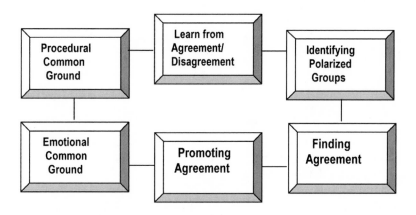

Figure 7.1.   An Outline for Common Ground

In some respects, this form of conflict resolution remains a part of many school leaders' definition of leadership.

In contrast to a more fact finding–conflict resolution style that seeks out differences is the mediation and conciliation style of leadership where common ground is established before trying to solve a school problem (Kosmoski and Pollack 2005). In this chapter, common ground is explored as a viable instrument for helping solve school-related problems. Through accepting the importance of both agreement and disagreement in schools, school leaders may gain a better understanding of those polarized people and groups who disagree.

It may be the establishment of common ground that allows a problem to be solved when people are too polarized to consider conflict resolution, or when school personnel have gone underground and indirectly talk about conflicts without directly solving them. In such cases, actively finding common ground can bring people together. Common ground makes the conflicts between people seem less overwhelming and less polarizing.

Establishing a foundation of common ground also may deter potential violence, where feelings of isolation and perceptions of overwhelming differences trap people into believing violence is justified (Saltmarsh, Robinson, and Davies 2012). For example, cultural and ethnic differences in schools should celebrate diversity, not be a dividing line where violence is possible. Common ground helps erase such dividing lines in schools. It strengthens diversity and other differences between people. It helps school leaders unite people, even when the school is in conflict. Common ground in schools looks for agreement, regardless of school personnel disagreements.

CASE STUDY

The problems between the Gonzales family and the Warren Public Schools were ongoing. Hector, the youngest member of the Gonzales family, had a learning disability, where the school developed an individual educational program (IEP) that allowed Hector inclusion into a regular fifth-grade classroom. Unfortunately, this was a problem based on conflict between Hector's teacher, Ms. Percy, and his parents, who felt that proper services were not being given to him.

This was evident at IEP meetings where the chairperson of the committee told Hector's parents that he needed to move to a more restricted environment in the school's resource room. Hector's parents protested that ongoing prejudice existed between Ms. Percy and Hispanic students. Removing him was not a matter of providing more personalized service. It was a matter of discrimination that existed between the school and the Hispanic community.

Tempers between the Gonzales family and the school had attracted numerous joiners to both sides of the problem. Hector's teacher, Ms. Percy, had complained to the principal of the school, and demanded the school back her up and remove Hector from the classroom. The Hispanic community sentiments spread to the classroom, where other students in Ms. Percy's class protested her treatment of them. By the time the conflict reached the desk of the superintendent of the school, both sides had "dug in" for a long legal battle. John, the school superintendent, realized this was more complicated than it first appeared, when asked to give direction to the dispute.

First of all, Hector received effective accommodations for tests, received help from a classroom assistant, and was maintaining passable scores in the fifth grade. The difficulty was in socializing with students from the mainstream culture, where disputes erupted and where Hector was accused of being the instigator.

John decided to discuss Hector's future with both the Gonzales family, Ms. Percy, and the chairperson of the IEP committee. He called all sides to meet with him, individually. During the discussion, it was agreed in all three meetings that whatever resolution took place would be in the best interest of Hector. It also became clear that the dispute was more than what procedures needed to be followed, but also what emotions were getting in the way of a fair and balanced discussion of Hector's future. It was also agreed that the dispute had gotten bigger than everyone expected, with others joining sides in the dispute for their own personal reasons and gains. Finally, it was decided that the type of dispute was about opposing points of view, and that strictly making a judgment or basing a decision only on school procedures could inflame the dispute rather than resolve it.

John took these points into consideration when he drew up a list of common ground between them:

- All agreed that whatever the resolution, it would be in the best interest of Hector.
- All agreed that frustration was getting in the way of a fair and balanced discussion.
- All agreed that the dispute had gotten bigger than both sides expected.
- All agreed that the dispute had gone beyond school procedures and that emotions were running high.

John composed a letter to all sides where he stated the above points and asked if mediation could take place between a representative from the IEP committee and Ms. Percy on one side, and the Gonzales family and a representative of their choice on the other (the Gonzales family brought their lawyer).

All sides agreed, and the mediation took place with a mediator from the state's special education mediation program. As it turned out, the mediation was highly emotional. However, the mediator established more common ground; namely, both agreed that communication had broken down, that looking for blame made things worse, that Hector had high anxiety and had trouble making friends, and that it was not the treatment of Hector's learning disability that was at issue. The IEP seemed to cover his needs. More important was the issue of how he could be successfully included in the classroom environment.

The final agreement was simple, yet inclusive. Ms. Percy created periods where the Hispanic community could plan cultural awareness sessions in her classroom, and Hector's parents agreed to allow him to work with both the resource room teachers and the school counselor in dealing with issues of cultural transitions and social anxiety. After the successful mediation, John concluded that without establishing a substantial amount of common ground the dispute might have ended in litigation, where people's emotions were overlooked, and where a legal judgment by the courts would only solve a portion of the problem.

COMMON GROUND AND SCHOOL CLIMATE

Learn from Agreement and Disagreement

Before common ground is possible in a school, leadership may need to establish with school personnel an understanding that agreement and disagreement have equal value. Such a position underlies the foundation inherent in any democratic institution. Sometimes this democratic principle gets lost or misinterpreted in schools. The idea that schools will improve when everyone remains in agreement usually denotes that disagreement has been marginalized, not viewed as productive, or not healthy for the school environment (Bellamy and Goodlad, 2008).

Effective leaders create a sense of democracy in the climate of a school when people believe they have the opportunity to disagree. Trying to deny disagreement in schools can create more dissent through feelings of oppression. As subtle as this concept may appear on the surface of people's consciousness, underneath may be trauma that is clearly understood.

For example, a student may quickly surmise when a teacher does not allow for disagreement. The student may search for answers that agree with the teacher's position, rather than risk disagreement. Or, the student may indirectly rebel with acts of resentment. Yet such an underlying experience is not exclusive with students. Teachers and other staff members may sense when leaders in schools openly state that they welcome disagreement, but in reality, they know it is *not* in one's best interest to disagree. Such an illusion of harmony can be experienced in specific schools, where on the surface the school climate seems harmonious, while just under the surface are resentments and unresolved conflicts polarizing the school (Brizendine 2005).

Effective Leadership

There is much that can be learned from accepting both agreement and disagreement in schools. Learning about a conflict requires as much understanding of how people disagree along with how they agree. In the case study, John wanted to learn from the dispute, but he realized that it was highly complex. Instead of only fact finding, he also looked for areas of agreement between Ms. Percy, the Gonzales family, and the special education teachers. He knew that it was important to send the message to everyone involved that agreement and disagreement had equal value. Instead of falling into the trap of deciding who was to blame, John looked for common ground.

In a dispute where there are differing points of view, as in the case study, having school leaders solely focusing on fact finding sends the wrong message, namely, "I am looking for who is right and who is wrong." Right and wrong are less important than "How do we solve this problem?" In the case study, John reduced the problem to a workable level through finding common ground between them, and placed those involved in a position to discuss the problem in mediation.

Using conciliatory skills for mending relationships can be a more productive leadership strategy than determining right from wrong. In conflicts where differing points of view are in dispute and no rules are broken, school leadership may learn more from finding agreement, rather than pinpointing disagreement.

Identifying Polarized Groups

When establishing common ground, it may require leaders to have a clear understanding of polarized individuals or groups working within schools. Such an effort is not intended to single out troublemakers or malcontents, but to acknowledge disagreement as an important part of a democratic process. Disagreements may be an opportunity to further improve the climate of a school, especially when these disagreements come from a constructive and growth-enhancing point of view.

Even if they do not, it still makes sense to understand those areas in schools that potentially have a negative effect on what schools stand for. It is more constructive for school leaders to agree to disagree with those in disagreement than to ignore the disagreement exists (Arif and Afshan 2009). In creating common ground, effective leaders need to establish that, 1.) disagreement is allowed and 2.) the leader has an awareness of the concerns of those in disagreement. These two points seem mandatory requirements if leaders are going to establish common ground in the climate of schools.

Effective Leadership

In the case study, at first glance, it seemed the dispute was between Ms. Percy and the Gonzales family. However, John took a more holistic view of the problem. He realized the Hispanic community was also involved, and that the dispute was based on problems surrounding the IEP committee. John identified all of the polarized groups involved in the dispute. It made no sense in finding agreement only to have some outside person or group of people sabotage it. In disputes based on differing points of view, it is more productive to find all of those who have a stake in the outcome of the dispute.

At this point, let us stop and ask some obvious questions. Why did John turn the dispute over to the State Special Education Mediation Program? As the leader of the school, why did *he not bring* all concerned parties together? John was smart enough to realize that he represented the school, and belonged to one of the polarized groups. This was not the type of dispute where the chief administrator made a judgment on who was right or wrong, according to the school's guidelines.

It was a highly emotional dispute that was getting bigger, and where one of the disputants was the school itself. School leaders cannot be responsible for finding a solution that is agreeable to everyone when they are part of the problem. Statewide Education Mediation Programs were designed to address such problems, and having a neutral, third-party mediator protects schools as well as, in this case, the family.

Finding Agreement

Identifying polarized groups in disagreement puts school leaders in a position to establish common ground that acknowledges agreements and disagreements. School leaders that advocate for democracy are now in a position to find common ground. At this point, it may be beneficial to ask the question, "In a practical sense, what does the term *common ground* mean for school leaders, and how does it improve the climate of a school?"

Simply put, common ground means *finding agreement in disagreement.* Instead of initially focusing on issues and concerns in disagreement, effective school leaders first establish agreement. Why is this important to the school's climate? The more agreement discovered between disagreeing parties the less polarization of these parties.

Many polarized groups work from the unchecked assumption that differences between them are enormous, overwhelming, and too volatile, and because of these beliefs, they seek safety with others who are in agreement with them. This becomes problematic for school leaders, based on polarized groups agreeing with each other but reluctant to find agreement with others outside their group. Finding common ground among these polarized groups "shrinks" the perception of disagreement being too enormous, or too overwhelming, or even too volatile (Blanchfield, Blanchfield and Ladd 2008).

The more agreement established in finding common ground among polarized groups in schools, the more manageable any disagreement. Common ground pulls people from their poles of safety to a more manageable center, where disagreement can be resolved effectively. Without establishing a working level of common ground, it becomes difficult for school leaders to allow for agreement and disagreement. Without common ground, the perception in a school climate falls more toward "us against them" rather than "let us work through our disagreements."

Effective Leadership

In the case study, John and the state special education mediator were instrumental in pointing out common ground that eventually made the dispute manageable for a successful resolution. All through the process, John and the mediator continually focused on finding common ground. It was the loss of common ground that polarized the dispute, where looking for blame became more important than solving the problem. Finding someone to blame can become the option of choice when emotions run high.

In this case, seeking out blame about who was right or wrong missed an important and initial issue of common ground, namely, "It is agreed that whatever resolution reached will be in the best interest of Hector." Regardless of who was to blame, John and the state mediator found common ground around Hector's future, and the success of the mediation needed to emphasize this point.

In disputes in schools where emotions run high, and where it is clear whether any rules were broken, school leadership should consider a more conciliation/mediation formula for resolving disputes. Sometimes an effective conciliator, as found with John in the case study, can help mend relationships enough so that polarized groups will consider talking to each other. In the case study, John became a successful conciliator by getting concerned parties to mediation.

However, John was also aware that others may perceive him as part of the problem. So he removed himself and deferred to a mediator. Sometimes referring interpersonal and highly emotional disputes, such as those found in many special education mediations, to an outside neutral third party shows an understanding of the problem, and is an example of democratic school leadership.

Promoting Agreement

It must be pointed out that finding common ground is not as effective if leaders in schools do not promote the importance of establishing common interests, or common points of view, throughout the school. Finding common ground can lose its importance if school leaders do not emphasize the benefits of working together in the climate of the school. This becomes most critical in schools where conflict is the major theme influencing the school climate. Sometimes, ineffective school leaders act as detectives by looking for conflict first while ignoring common ground. The message sent to school personnel can be that the leader is looking for "what is wrong with us" rather than "what positive forces we have in common."

Finding common ground can reduce negative sentiments among entire groups, while making conflicts more manageable in their resolution. For example, we may be reminded of schools where gossip and innuendo go a long way in promoting the polarization of a school. At the heart of this polarization are those individuals who continuously promote the use of negative communication, regardless of its impact. The statement "misery loves company" is not far from what happens when negativity reinforces polarized groups at the expense of the school's climate.

Many school leaders combat negativity by boosting morale and acting positively. Yet neither of these directly addresses the problems inherent in a polarized group of people. Beyond being positive leaders are informed leaders who can point out and promote the common ground between those in the school, and then use that common ground to bring polarized groups together (Tyack 2007). Boosting a school's morale may be an activity that helps improve the feelings of those associated with the school, but finding common ground may put leaders in a position to depolarize a polarized school climate. Without specifically addressing the issue of polarization, a school is vulnerable to any new polarizing conflict that may threaten the climate of the school.

Effective Leadership

The case study can stand as an example of a school leader who looked beyond any given dispute and considered the climate where these disputes were taking place. In the case study, all eyes were watching to see whether John would take sides and blame someone for the problem. It was up to John to attempt a resolution that was perceived as fair to all concerned groups. If he had only used the skill of fact finding and then rendered a decision as the chief school administrator, this may have caused more conflict, not less. This case study points out how an effective school leader can include a diversity of opinions when emotions are running high, and the outcome of a dispute may affect all those trying to maintain an identity in the school.

It also points out two problems that may occur when one is sometimes overlooked by ineffective school leaders. The first problem is attending to those affected by the dispute. The second is how the outcome of the dispute impacts the school climate. In the case study, John had as much of a school climate problem to resolve as an interpersonal problem between disputing parties. Without establishing common ground, such problems as found in the case study can escalate into racial, ethnic, and discrimination problems. The explosive nature of conflict, such as in the case study, may need a holistic understanding where common ground is established not only for the disputants, but also for those in the school waiting to see if there will be a fair and balanced outcome.

Emotional Common Ground

In order to specify the types of common ground that are relevant to improving school climate, the next two sections are devoted to that end. Emotional common ground is based on those emotions that people in schools can agree are directly affecting the climate of a school. For example, in a highly functional school climate, one may expect to find such emotions as compassion, trust, and generosity.

However, in a dysfunctional school climate, such emotions as resentment, apathy, or anxiety may be setting the emotional tone when entering and working in the school. School leaders who find common ground in how people are feeling and have others in the school agree to this emotional common ground create an opportunity for a meaningful discussion around disagreements and problems.

Also, by discussing emotional common ground and having people agree, it leads the school into more specific discussions on emotional differences. For example, if leaders establish agreement among school personnel that resentment in the school is a problem, then it becomes easier to discuss different reasons for the resentment, such as communication breakdown or differences over curriculum or confusion over school rules. For mediators and conciliators, establishing emotional common ground has been a necessity when dealing with, for example, angry mobs or anxiety-ridden workplaces (Doherty and Guyler 2008).

In the same manner, school leaders can establish common ground that creates an emotional framework for how people function and behave within schools. For example, trying to resolve an issue over school rules regarding discipline in the classroom may elicit a more positive outcome if there is agreement that discussing discipline produces a *considerable amount of anxiety*. By establishing emotional common ground, even based on the topic of anxiety, school leaders work from a position of agreement, as opposed to coping with each person's individual emotional state.

Effective Leadership

There are school leaders who avoid emotions or overlook them when people are in dispute, and primarily focus on school procedures. Such a stance assumes that the primary responsibility of any school leader is management. However, conflict in schools may promote different priorities that include reestablishing emotional relationships among those in schools. In the case study, John acted as a conciliator and tried to mend relationships between the school and the Gonzales family, at least enough so that they would agree to mediation.

Some may ask, "What happens if they did not agree to a formal mediation?" In this case, John probably would continue doing "shuttle diplomacy" back and forth between all parties involved and find enough common ground until a solution seemed reasonable and fair. However, in this case, he probably would focus more on emotions than procedures, especially on their anger and anxiety.

Emotions are at the heart of any dispute, and in emotionally charged disputes, emotional common ground helps to defuse feelings that inhibit resolution. For example, in the case study, John had all parties agree that the *dispute had become frustrating*, and that blaming each other did not help. By John acknowledging the emotional common ground of frustration, he openly declared that sharing each person's frustration was more acceptable than blaming each other.

By establishing emotional common ground, John allowed emotions to be expressed, but within the guidelines of a fair and equal conflict resolution process. Understanding specific emotions such as frustration, resentment, anxiety, and revenge make the use of emotional common ground a preferred practice when resolving school-related disputes.

Procedural Common Ground

Procedural common ground does not necessarily mean that everyone involved agrees on the procedures taking place in a school. It may mean everyone involved agrees that procedures are important. For example, a leader may start a discussion surrounding what procedures are important regarding school safety. An effective school leader may first establish a common ground agreement that school safety rules are important, and this may set the tone for discussing differences in procedures.

This example, at first glance, seems obvious that people would agree that school safety rules are important. However, having everyone openly agreeing on procedural common ground places the leader in a better position to return to this common ground when disagreements become unmanageable.

Let us try another example of procedural common ground. Two English teachers were fighting over which curriculum was best for eleventh-grade English students. Their ongoing disagreement had gotten out of control, where each teacher had a group of polarized faculty backing up their positions. The school leader negotiated between these two teachers; however, both English teachers constantly drifted off to the ideas that supported their position.

Finally, the leader established this important piece of procedural common ground. "Do you both agree that whatever curriculum you develop will be in the best interest of the students?" After they agreed, the conversation shifted from what was in the best interest of the two English teachers to what was in the best interest of the students. This one piece of procedural common ground solved the dispute, while dissolving the polarized groups on either side.

Effective Leadership

In the case study, John's first response was not an attempt at fact finding or rendering a judgment. He first established procedural common ground with all disputing parties. He had all parties agree that whatever resolution was agreed upon it would be in the best interest of Hector. He also found agreement that the dispute had gotten bigger than "school procedures," and that an outside mediator was best suited for dispute resolution. Sometimes, creative dispute resolution is not only about finding an optimal resolution, but in finding the most effective procedures to render an optimal resolution.

In schools, some disputes based on rules and procedures require school leaders to render a decision. In other disputes, where emotions run high, it is the leader's responsibility to help mend relationships and reconcile emotionally charged parties. And, sometimes, it is a combination of both, where procedures and emotions require leaders to oversee agreements that address both with equal importance.

In the case study, John effectively conciliated the dispute by bringing all parties together, while the mediator helped them with an agreement that considered procedures such as a culture-awareness session in Ms. Percy's classroom. Also considered were emotions, where Hector received counseling for social anxiety and difficult transitions.

SCHOOL VIOLENCE AND COMMON GROUND

This chapter demonstrates the potential for violence escalating even in minor disputes. For example, in the case study, what appeared on the surface as a school-related adjustment with a student with a learning disability almost turned into a community-wide problem of discrimination, emotional abuse, and possible litigation. Potential violence is possible in any school-related dispute that has some form of history attached to it, such as found in the case study; namely, family, culture, and learning disabilities.

For example, in 2007, it was reported by the National Center for Educational Statistics (NCES 2007) that escalating conflict was more likely in schools that had a higher minority student population. Though it is hard to measure the emotional investment that goes into these types of disputes, it becomes understandable why emotions run high and why the primary issue that needs resolution may be the escalating emotions between minority groups and the school. In the case study, John's role went beyond upholding the procedures of the school.

Under the circumstances found in the case study, an overemphasis on school procedures, at the expense of having an opportunity to express emotions, may be perceived as hiding behind school procedures in order to protect school personnel. Such perceptions may escalate the problem into matters of race, ethnicity, and inequality.

The popular sentiment for some school leaders is that schools need to be places of safety, where strict procedures are adhered to, for possible violent attacks on schools (Browne-Dianis 2011). Yet many of the disputes in schools do not originate from outside the school, but in misunderstandings within the school that polarize people into groups. Tolerance can generate less violence than no tolerance at all. Finding common ground is a tolerant method for reducing violence in schools. It brings people together based on their similarities, not their differences. It minimizes conflict by demonstrating agreement, not disagreement, and it makes any resolution of a problem more manageable and reasonable.

It also makes the statement that "we can learn from each other, about each other, before violence is necessary." In the case study, both sides demonstrated unknown intentions and fears about the opposing side. Finding emotional common ground helped to alleviate their fears, while procedural common ground helped clarify each side's intentions. Finding common ground can be one of the most important methods available for maintaining a peaceful school. When school leaders look for similarities before exploring differences, it sends a message to all involved in the climate of the school that "we are more similar to each other than you may think, and it is through our similarities that conflict will be resolved, in spite of our differences."

SUMMARY

In this chapter, we discussed the concept of finding common ground, and how such a skill can redefine school leadership. In certain disputes, common ground can be more effective than management of school rules and procedures. This is not to say that discipline policies, illegal possession of drugs and firearms, and numerous other issues do not require procedures and the school leaders who are willing to enforce them. What this chapter reveals is that not all conflict in schools can be resolved through procedures alone.

Emotionally charged disputes, with legitimate opposing viewpoints, may require school leaders to be conciliators or mediators when resolving disputes, especially when high emotions are the main ingredient. The case study in this chapter is an example of such a conflict, where falling back on procedures may have escalated the conflict, rather than reduced it. Furthermore, the case study revealed that effective school leaders in these types of disputes are as much concerned with the school climate as they are with the presenting dispute.

Finding common ground becomes the great neutralizer in emotionally charged disputes. It allows opposing parties to realize they are emotionally in agreement, even when agreement is based on anger or frustration. Finding common ground can be the emotional starting point for more specific issues in disagreement. It can shrink the dispute to a workable level where it becomes clear what needs resolution.

The case study is an example of a dispute that had high-stakes ramifications if handled incorrectly. It was a dispute where the most important element was in finding enough common ground. After establishing common ground, the agreement was simplified; namely, learn about each other through cultural awareness and get Hector counseling. However, getting to that resolution took an effective school leader who could establish the common ground needed for talking to each other.

Violence in schools can be acts of premeditation, as found in numerous school shootings, whether by gangs, disgruntled teachers and students, or outside, deranged individuals. Or, it can be found in the emotional reactions to disputes that were inappropriately addressed by the school and its leaders. In both cases, finding common ground lessens violence in schools. It is a method based on the power of agreement, not disagreement. It seems a prerequisite for any school leader that is placed in the position of resolving conflict in schools.

Chapter Eight

Humor

There are several different functions for humor in a school beyond creating laughter and amusement. As we will see in this chapter, humor creates common ground within the climate of a school while also reducing stress (Booth-Butterfield and Wanzer 2010). However, being specific about the type of humor being expressed is also an important consideration for effective school leadership. Negative humor such as sexual joking, teasing about student intelligence; laughing at stereotypes; vulgar language; and humor relating to race, religion, and politics rarely develops cohesion in schools.

Rather, it isolates people into noticeably smaller groups where prejudice, unfortunately, becomes the common ground. Positive humor, such as jokes about school activities, lighthearted teasing of colleagues about school-relat-

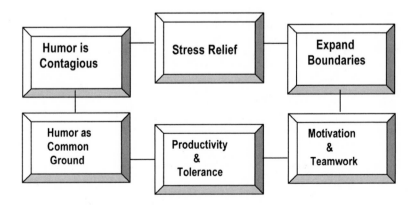

Figure 8.1.   An Outline for Humor

ed topics, the telling of humorous school stories, and making fun of yourself can bring the school together in forming positive common ground.

Humor can also function as an effective coping mechanism in times of crisis or when a school-wide experience spreads anxiety, anger, and jealousy through a school. For school leaders, the benefits of humor are sometimes overlooked, whether the humor is intentional, as in making faculty and staff find humor in a difficult decision affecting them, or in unintentional humor where school leaders make mistakes and laugh at themselves. Humor makes the climate of a school more relaxed, manageable, enjoyable, and interesting (Jonas 2009). Also, humor may be an opportunity for the school climate to incorporate a more multicultural sense of humor (Ziv 1988).

In this regard, humor can expand the boundaries of what is possible by inclusion of individual differences in a more nonaggressive or lighthearted manner. One could speculate that humor has connections to democracy, where disagreement can be tempered when leaders do not take themselves too seriously.

CASE STUDY

Nancy was a nationally recognized authority in mental health counseling when she took the position of director of the counseling center at a major university in the Northeast. Her accomplishments were well noted. She had published numerous positively reviewed books, and as a former college professor, she not only understood counseling theory but also counseling practice. The university had convinced her to take the position as a way of spending her remaining years before retiring from the school.

Though a bit intimidated by her accomplishments, the counseling staff welcomed her with respect and dignity. They believed she was the correct choice for the fifteen counselors, who seemed barraged with constant conflict by the demands of students being in crisis. Their hope was that she could give direction to a staff that seemed exhausted and had recently been attacking each other through gossip, blaming, and complaints about how much they hated coming to work.

Early in her tenure as the director, she would show up at each counselor's office when they were not counseling and announce that she was "drifting." When asked, "What in the world is drifting?" she said, "It is the ability to walk into another's office with no purpose or intention." She simply said that she was "drifting around." This invariably made the counselors laugh, and with time, they began to "drift" back. For some unknown reason, drifting around had taken hold, and the stress levels of the counselors began to decrease. Instead of the director coming to each person's office for business, she just showed up.

The interesting part of these visits was the differences each meeting produced regarding relevant conversations. Sometimes in a meeting they did discuss specific cases, while other times it was a chance to vent on just about anything. On occasions, the conversation turned to family and friends or special events. It did not matter because drifting needed no purpose or intent. What did become evident was how the emotional climate of the counseling center became less tense and became more comfortable.

Nancy knew that conflict is neither good nor bad, especially in a counseling center. Conflict and counseling go hand in hand, and when one of the counselors received her first "button," everyone seemed shocked. When tensions got high and the counselors began noticing that someone was "losing it," Nancy would give them a button. For example, after one of the counselors complained about her clients for what seemed to others like days on end, Nancy gave her a button that said, "Help Stop Global Whining."

At first, the counselors did not know what to think about getting a button until Nancy started wearing a button that said, "Big Mean Counseling Machine." Again, as with the practice of drifting, a person could get a button for being annoying, or could receive one that pointed out a positive side of their personality. The interesting theme was how Nancy did not give out buttons unless a conflict was in the air. Instead of lecturing, advising, questioning, or analyzing the behavior of the counselors, she allowed conflict to be approached with humor. For the counselors, they recognized the humor but also the message. It was Nancy's way of allowing the counselors to resolve their own conflict before she had to step in as their director.

One other characteristic may need mentioning. After six months of Nancy being the director of the counseling center, one of the counselors at a team meeting said to her, "I knew that you were a highly respected author and practitioner in the field of counseling, and also a respected professor, but I had no idea how funny and self-deprecating you could be in front of us. Thank you!" Nancy answered her, "We are all in this together. Being a counselor takes as much humility as it does expertise. Without humor we are less productive, less motivated and less effective. We need to take our work seriously, but we also need to balance it with moments when humor helps us survive the seriousness of our work."

These words reflected the philosophy now present in the counseling center that all were engaged in serious work, but our effectiveness increased if we did not take ourselves too seriously. As it turned out, Nancy took counseling very seriously. She had constant in-service workshops on suicide prevention, crisis counseling, addictions and disorders counseling, multicultural issues, and many others. She stated, "I want you to be 'superstars' in the counseling field," and she held all involved to a high standard. Yet she also understood the dynamics of the profession, its trauma and exhaustion. She used humor as a method to acknowledge a more democratic view of the counseling profession.

HUMOR AND SCHOOL CLIMATE

Stress Relief

One of the benefits for leaders using humor in schools, and probably one the major reasons to use humor, is its remarkable ability to relieve stress (Palestini 2012). Humor affects the brain by releasing endorphins that help in stabilizing a person's mood, thus leading to calming behavior (Morrison 2012). In stressful situations, humor acts as a neutralizer of negative emotion. It lightens the mood and allows leaders to discuss issues with others that may be too volatile without humor.

Humor empowers others to join in and be a part of the discussion. It reduces the power imbalances among school personnel by creating rapport, where others feel a sense of equality (Jonas 2009). It also gives leaders an opportunity to laugh at themselves, or be openly vulnerable as the butt of a joke.

School leaders may consider humor appropriate in a style of leadership where maintaining a healthy school climate is a clearly established concept. For example, an authoritarian leadership style, where leaders are mostly the "rule enforcers," may find humor a dangerous and risky activity to use in schools. However, democratic leaders who are involved in human relations activities and make an effort to include others in problem solving may find humor indispensable.

Humor can keep an open line of communication between leaders and staff, regardless of the stress level or conflict (Ryan and Rottmann 2009). Humor not only helps in the reduction of stressful situations, it also may change peoples' appraisals of stressful situations, while having an impact on their reaction to them.

Effective Leadership

In the case study, we saw humor being used by Nancy who understood the conflict and possible derision present in her staff. For example, her making up a term for just showing up at people's offices and calling it "drifting" was a statement to all counselors that "I am open to whatever you want to talk about, but I have no specific purpose behind my visit." In a climate where democracy is an important goal, being open for any topic as opposed to constant mandates and directives can reduce stress and improve the climate of the organization.

Nancy was smart enough to recognize that visiting with no purpose gave her counselors an opportunity to create their purpose for the visit, one where they were free to let their comments go in whatever direction was important to them. Through humor, Nancy opened the door for serious, lighthearted, or informational conversations to take place, all of which helped to reduce stress in the counseling center.

Leadership that does not find ways for people to express themselves runs the risk of drifting into a climate of anxiety and stress, where the ability to remain resilient in one's professional role may be less conceivable. In the case study, we saw a school leader who understood the potential for stress reduction, while building resiliency through the use of humor.

Expand Boundaries

Here is a subtle, yet important, point to make about humor's effect on the structure and boundaries of a school. All institutional situations have boundaries that affect the school, whether spoken, as in "no smoking in the work-place," or unspoken, as in "we share with colleagues when in conflict." Such boundaries apply directly to the climate of a school. When there is anxiety, resentment, anger, revenge, jealousy, and other problems, the boundaries of an institution may shrink.

In other words, people in the school are more afraid to be outspoken, critical, productive, and creative. The boundaries may shrink because what-ever is causing the conflict begins to dominate people's thinking, leaving other functions of the school less likely to be perceived with a sense of freedom or trust. In this manner, negative emotions can have a strong social influence on the boundaries and functioning of schools (Gass and Seiter 2007).

Humor can act as a positive social influence on the climate of schools. For example, if the school leader announces that there will be cutbacks in staff in the next week, anxiety may shrink the boundaries of the school based on discussions regarding layoffs. Again, such a conflict makes most people tense and uncertain, but it also changes how they view what can be said or accomplished during this uncertainty.

Humor will not necessarily change the anxiety of individuals who believe their position or salary is in jeopardy, but it may expand the boundaries of what can be discussed so that people can openly talk about their anxiety or concerns (Vlieghe, Simons, and Masschelein 2010).

School leaders are not in a position to take away each person's emotional response to trauma, conflict, or outside pressures. However, they can be effective in expanding the boundaries of their schools so that others feel safe in expressing their concerns. Humor lightens things up and gives people more room to process conflict and work through their problems.

Effective Leadership

In the case study, Nancy made a concerted effort to expand the boundaries of the counseling center by injecting humor into her leadership style. When she gave out "buttons" to the counselors, she expanded the boundaries of what could be discussed openly among the staff. Through humor, she created an unspoken rule that we can laugh at our shortcomings while also being proud of our character traits. She expanded the boundaries of acceptable conversation in the counseling center.

She realized that being too serious shrinks the boundaries of what is possible. In conflict situations, effective school leaders may have a responsibility to expand the boundaries of an institution in order to buffer the blow of too much stress, anxiety, or resentment. Humor is an indirect method to expand these boundaries. It allows people within the climate of the organization to not take themselves and others too seriously, thus allowing their work to be taken more seriously. Expanding the boundaries of a workplace setting may be an important responsibility of democratic leadership. Humor may be a method for accomplishing this goal.

Motivation and Teamwork

The leader who said, "Fear is the great motivator," was not talking about a democratic style of leadership. Motivating the school climate is considered a mandatory characteristic of effective democratic leaders, and fear rarely motivates anyone (Siddique et al. 2011). If you think about it, even in more authoritarian leadership styles, fear still is not a great motivator. Fear may create compliance to the demands of leaders, where others fear consequences, but that is not motivation. It means they are afraid of the consequences. Conversely, humor may be the direct opposite of fear and can become a motivating factor in creating the proper environment where democracy can take place.

Humor can generate a constructive mood while it defines the situation as safe from reprimands and punishment. Effective leaders in schools can gain more individual motivation from the use of humor than fear. Humor draws people away from the source of stress rather than toward it. People seem more willing to be motivated and join a team when they feel the team is approachable, and leaders of the team are open to good and bad news (Holmes and Marra 2006).

This becomes important when there are dissenters in schools who resist most discussions of motivation or team efforts. These may be dissenters who want to maintain the status quo and protect their "turf." Approaching dissenters, or other team members for that matter, in a somber and humorless manner may kill motivation and teamwork. Being part of a team and being motivated by the team may require a sense of shared conviction along with a school climate that allows for individual differences. Humor can help people recognize and accept these differences (Curtis and O'Connell 2011).

Effective Leadership

In the case study, Nancy gave a button to one of her counselors that stated "Help Stop Global Whining." She gave herself a button and wore it stating, "Lean, Mean, Counseling Machine." How can these gestures create motivation and teamwork? We have seen in previous chapters, examples of leadership that included concepts such as empowerment, assertiveness, and common ground, which help in the creation of, freedom and clarity and help to bring people together. Leaders who can laugh at themselves allow humor to enter the realm of possibilities when trying to motivate and create teamwork in people. In the case study, the message sent by Nancy was that "we are all in this together."

By giving out buttons, she laughed at herself while creating a new activity called "drifting." Through subtle forms of humor, she re-created the climate at the counseling center where there were remedies for a lack of motivation, and where she stated that "we can find ways of dealing with our exhaustion, together." It may be the old saying "misery loves company" that has its positive side when humor is injected into the conversation.

Productivity and Tolerance

"Productive people are happy people." "Happy people are more tolerant of conflict, stress, and change." Both of these comments help define a leadership style that considers humor as an important ingredient in maintaining an effective school climate. Humor can help to break down the old industrial, dictatorial, "top-down" leadership style of another era (Simplicio 2011). In an information age where leadership is based on problem solving more than on controlling a group of people, humor helps solve problems, making others more productive and tolerant of these problems (Penney 2011).

A democratic style of leadership that values humor demonstrates the potential for expanding the boundaries of what is possible by making problems more tolerable. In a school climate, where the productivity of faculty, staff, and students is a primary goal, the maintenance of tolerant and productive schools can be reinforced through humor.

This is not to say that leaders cannot have high standards for productivity in the classroom, curriculum, or any other related theme. However, humor can promote tolerance and create a more productive place to work than one that lacks humor. This concept is important today where school officials are barraged with tragic examples such as school shootings, sexual misconduct

of staff, or multicultural outbreaks of violence. Such events are serious re-
minders of what can happen when *productivity and tolerance are not viewed
equally.*

Such events may challenge overreactions from leaders, where they re-
strict the rights of staff and students based on these events. One event should
not be the reason for negative changes in the climate of a school. More
democratic leaders separate these tragic events from the school climate by
restoring productivity and by emphasizing a tolerance for each other. Sometimes effective leaders use humor to restore the climate of a school after a
crisis has happened, or when an imminent crisis is in the air.

Effective Leadership

Before considering effective leadership in a school setting that promotes
productivity and tolerance, let us take a moment to consider a setting that
demands productivity but is intolerant. For example, in the case study, when
Nancy became director of the counseling center, the counselors were not
being productive and were intolerant of their work. The constant demands on
their time and energy left them hating the thought of coming to work. In a
sense, they were asked to increase their productivity to meet the demand of
clients needing help, while slowly becoming more intolerant of their roles as
counselors.

Considering the case study, some leaders may put an emphasis on the
counselors being more productive and having better success with those clients being counseled. Nancy understood the connection between productivity
and tolerance. If she could help her staff become more tolerant, and therefore
more resilient, she believed productivity would follow. Humor increases our
ability to tolerate stressful circumstances, and it allows us to be more productive when in these circumstances.

Humor as Common Ground

Let us continue the discussion from chapter 7 on developing common
ground, but where humor is used in difficult situations found in the climate of
a school. Here is an example. When a tragedy happens such as a teen suicide,
school shooting, or heated arguments among faculty members, different factions in the school can become polarized into groups. In other words, different groups may have different opinions, responses, or reactions to these
events, separating them from others.

Again, school leaders cannot inappropriately use humor in directly dealing with such serious matters. The expectation from everyone involved is for
leadership to take these issues seriously and deal with them professionally.
However, what happens after leaders deal with the problems effectively,

seriously, and professionally? How do these leaders pick up the pieces of the school climate and restore a positive atmosphere?

Humor may be one of the more effective methods in restoring common ground among a polarized group of people (Hurren 2005). Humor may be the common ground needed after a tragic incident that brings people together and allows them to heal. Humor may be the leader's way of saying, "We need closure, and we need to reunite for the purpose of teaching and learning." Obviously, using humor as common ground in tragic circumstances requires a sense of timing and tact. There is a time for crisis intervention, and there should be a time for healing.

Humor makes sense when trying to heal a school climate that has experienced too much trauma. However, humor should not be considered valuable for only major traumas in schools. Blow-ups can happen in schools, sometimes on a daily basis. Again, humor becomes important after the explosions are dealt with, and when the focus is on restoring the school climate. Humor can be viewed as a democratic practice for finding common ground that brings people back together.

Effective Leadership

In the case study, Nancy realized her counseling staff had experienced too much trauma, and they were now taking it out on each other. She understood they were polarized and had lost their common ground. She sought out common ground through what appeared to be meaningless rituals. Any form of common ground became important when her staff was polarized, exhausted, and in need of direction. Meaningless as these rituals may have appeared, they became safe, comfortable methods for reestablishing a sense of unity among the group. In a climate that has lost its common ground, any form of it can restore the climate of a school or institution.

Humor is one of many rituals that can be established to this end, along with such activities as socializing after work, going on retreats, and taking an interest in outside activities not connected to work. As an example, in the case study, the ritual of "drifting" opened the door for discussions around these and other issues. It was a humorous method that allowed common ground to emerge within the creativity of the staff, who then supplied purpose and meaning to these visits.

Humor Is Contagious

The art of leadership includes leading by example. Leadership is more about doing something than talking about it. Effective leaders who believe in democracy set the tone, create the ground rules, and define the boundaries of a school climate. Yet more important, democratic school leaders create an atmosphere where people can interact with each other (Ingram and Cangemi 2012). Highly judgmental leaders may be noted for a school climate filled with anxiety, guilt, and resentment, where people are judged, not heard, and where evaluation becomes the mode of operation that supersedes effective communication.

Such a climate can be contagious, and it may be a matter of time when anxiety, resentment, and overevaluation become the perceptions of students, parents, faculty, and staff. The climate of a school is not static, rigid, or permanent. It is dynamic, flexible, and contagious. It spreads! For example, you are a teacher who feels happy and productive and you enter the Teacher's Room at your school, only to experience negative, resentful, gossiping colleagues. How long is it before your happiness and positive outlook are affected? School leaders may have the responsibility in making sure the negative attitude of the Teacher's Room does not spread to the rest of the school.

Humor is one way of addressing this problem without directly causing more negative feelings. For example, leaders could enter the Teacher's Room and lighten the conversation, or call attention to the frustration of working with so many different types of students, or share humorous examples from the leaders' past about the topic of discussion. Whatever the method, leaders can intentionally enter any given negative and unproductive situation in a school and plant the seeds of humor. Humor can be as contagious as fear and anxiety, and it can become a method for expanding the former in order to minimize the latter.

Effective Leadership

In the case study, Nancy was aware of how the climate at the counseling center was in jeopardy based on the increased demand from student counseling problems at the university. She was also aware that signs of lateral violence were now being acted out between staff members. Pointing out the escalating nature of lateral violence becomes critical when nonparticipants may still be affected through apathy, anxiety, and trauma. In the case study, Nancy controlled the spread of lateral violence through forms of humor. As stated above, anger, resentment, and revenge can be highly contagious, affecting the climate of a school, and it can escalate into more serious forms of violence.

It was unlikely that the counselors at the counseling center would demonstrate escalating forms of violence, but they may look for another job, do poorly in their present job, or develop a negative reputation for their insensitivity. Humor can be an effective form of restoring a climate contaminated by lateral violence. It quickly takes the pressure off a highly stressful set of circumstances. In the case study, Nancy defused the escalating conflict at the counseling center by using her different, yet effective, sense of humor.

SCHOOL VIOLENCE AND HUMOR

As stated in the beginning of this chapter, certain types of humor can relieve stress, expand boundaries, and create common ground, while others can do the opposite: laughing at prejudice, bullying, and making fun of someone at their expense. In these cases, humor becomes a form of abuse, where the exploitation of power through humor creates a lack of sensitivity or an indifference to those who are the focus of negative humor (Kirsh and Kuiper 2003).

Unfortunately, expressions of negative humor can be a breeding ground for violence in schools, and it may be the perception of negative humor by school leaders that makes these leaders appear ineffective (Decker and Rotondo 2001). It also may be the indifference found in negative humor that may go undetected by school leaders who do not have an understanding of the importance of humor.

In the case study, Nancy used humor to combat lateral violence; however, she had to be careful that her methods were not taken as condescending or elitist. She was not indifferent to the feelings of others, but she helped them express their sentiments and feelings through the use of humor. Her intent was to expand the boundaries of what was possible while not putting anyone down. This can lead us to an understanding that the intentions behind being humorous may be as important as humorous behavior (Palestini 2012).

We know people who use forms of joking and sarcasm to put others down, and when confronted they say, "I was only joking." In the role of school leader, it may be important to make one's intentions clear. In the case study, Nancy gave buttons to draw out the counselors to talk about their problems, but she also displayed a button where she laughed at herself, thereby allowing others to also find humor in their working conditions.

In today's schools, the lines between humor that heals and humor that creates forms of violence may need further scrutiny. For example, cyberbullying may provide entertainment for bullies who use humor to hurt others. Thinking of humorous ways to insult someone or embarrass them becomes less difficult when one is not directly facing them. Events of being ridiculed under the disguise of humor has caused numerous incidents of deaths and suicides (El-Ghobashy 2010). School leaders may need a better understanding of positive and negative humor in an Information Age. Making jokes or laughing at someone becomes a different experience than helping them find humor in difficult and conflict-oriented experiences.

SUMMARY

Humor makes sense for leaders who espouse democratic forms of leadership based on its ability to relieve stress while creating common ground. In this chapter, we saw the experience of Nancy, and how she worked with her staff in resolving the conflicts that accumulated at the university counseling center. It may not be the methods she used, or the personality she conveyed to her staff, that was most important. Not everyone is humorous in the same way.

More important, it was the intentions behind her humor that made a difference with her staff. In some unconscious way, they knew she was trying to reach them and heal the climate of the counseling center. Her intentions were to lead, but not in a manner that increased a toxic environment. Rather, it was to do so in one that reduced it. Her focus was not on the counselors increasing productivity, but in learning to tolerate difficult times through the use of humor. She brought the group together by using humor as their common ground.

Creating structure and pointing the direction taken in any institution is the responsibility found in numerous forms of leadership. Humor makes it more tolerable and exciting to abide by specific institutional structures and the direction leaders want to take. In the case study, Nancy built a new direction for the counselors to follow, and it was structured around her sense of humor. Through her actions, she helped heal the counseling center and made it more productive. She went against the common practice of fact finding what was wrong with the counseling center, and she came up with a step-by-step plan to change the center's direction.

She created an environment where humor was acceptable, and where the problems inhibiting productivity and motivation could emerge. Effective school leadership is as much about implementing the correct process to connect with other human beings as the correct procedures for governing them. In the case study, the process of healing began through the use of humor.

Chapter Nine

Critical Thinking

One of the foundations connected to democratic school leadership is to engender critical thinking into the climate of schools. Critical thinking for school leaders can be defined as a thoughtful, open-minded approach that considers different points of view based on the accuracy found in arguments or opinions of others. Critical thinking involves accurate reasoning and honesty, while considering all possibilities and eliminating biases (Goodwin and Sommervold 2012).

More democratic leaders will ask questions, have a sense of curiosity, examine beliefs and opinions, and weigh them against facts. Critical thinkers will admit to a lack of understanding and will adjust to a point of view when new information is found. In these leadership skills, critical thinkers still

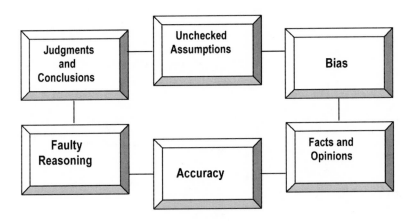

Figure 9.1.   An Outline for Critical Thinking

practice an open form of democracy by carefully listening to others, while giving constructive feedback (Lipman 2003).

In the following chapter, we will consider those characteristics that help school leaders create a climate that includes critical thinking and points out what can happen to the climate of a school when more insular thinking takes place. Conflict and violence in schools can be created by the thinking of its leaders. Unchecked assumptions based on biases of reactionary leaders can set the tone for a school filled with problems. Reactionary leaders can create indirect gossip and rumors in the climate of a school based on unchecked assumptions, where faulty reasoning can lead to violent behavior.

Leadership that believes in democracy needs a thorough understanding of critical thinking in order to uphold democratic principles such as empowerment, assertiveness, and finding common ground (Northouse 2012). All of these may require a leader who has accurately thought through how to enact these principles. For example, prejudice in schools is as much a critical-thinking problem as it is a multicultural one. Even those leaders who declare equality and diversity may find their beliefs compromised by being unable to think critically about the conflicts presented to them.

CASE STUDY

Bullying was rampant at Star Middle School, and the school district was looking for new ideas for combating out-of-control student behavior. The school was located in an inner-city community where it was assumed that violence was common, and the bullying taking place was one example of a community in decline. The assumption made by school leaders was that in order to stop bullying and other potential violence, a strict form of punishment was necessary. Beyond the metal detectors and locker searches was a zero-tolerance policy based on punishment and rewards. Students were rewarded for positive behavior, but they faced suspension for negative behavior, especially bullying.

Tolerance among school leaders was wearing thin. Each time a major bullying incident took place, the school's leaders reacted by restricting more school privileges for all students. Unfortunately, this allowed the bullies of the school an opportunity to create more victims. It was not only the bullies who were getting punished, but also the victims. The zero-tolerance policy did not discriminate. Anyone involved in an incident that broke school rules faced some form of punishment in the school.

In contrast to the bullying policy was the constant emphasis by school leaders on respecting the rights of other students. Yet the school leaders did little in allowing respectful participation in the life of the school. Constant rewarding of those selected few for not breaking the rules did little in creating any sense of social responsibility in the rest of the students. Actually, the opposite was more the case. Constantly rewarding a select group of students motivated them to get rewarded, while they ignored any commitment to being generous or respectful to others.

They were focused on the rewards rather than developing a social conscience. More important, the punishment that came from the zero-tolerance policy took precedent over students respecting each other. Punishment created compliance for short periods of time and taught students what was wrong to do, but it did little in helping students respect the rights of others.

Clara was a newly hired eighth-grade teacher at Star Middle School who had a strong commitment to democratic principles, and she included these principles in her social studies lesson plans. Though she held no leadership position, it was only a matter of time before others were taking notice of the sense of community, cultural acceptance, and ethical development in her classes.

She was dedicated to having her students be individuals of character, not only in her classroom but also in their community. Her goal was to create a classroom climate that included family, school, and community. She wanted to socially influence her students at all levels. For her, the school's efforts to gain respect required critical thinking that went beyond the present guidelines of the school.

Over the next few years, she slowly instituted policies in her classroom that defined respect as more than an abstract concept. She made an effort to critically think through what respect entailed at Star Middle School. The following are some of her efforts:

- She developed cooperative activities in the community through service learning, in developing a sense of responsibility, and in connection to the community as a whole.
- She encouraged discussions concerning aspects of school life and how to properly interact with other people in an appropriate manner.
- She encouraged students to critically think about social issues as they appeared in the curriculum.
- She established parent support groups to find common ground on ethical and moral issues relating to her curriculum.
- She encouraged self-discipline through cooperative interaction between students in the classroom.
- She provided for forms of student self-discipline such as peer mediation so students could help students, while developing critical-thinking and communication skills.

It may be that Star Middle School was lucky, or school leaders recognized a plan that was working. Regardless, they began instituting Clara's plans for the entire school. Over time, an interesting phenomenon took place. As respect for each other increased, bullying behavior decreased. Though Clara was not a recognized leader in the school, her critical-thinking skills helped define how to gain respect in a school. By including parents, community, and students in her plans, she used those affected by bullying to socially influence the development of a respectful school climate.

CRITICAL THINKING AND SCHOOL CLIMATE

Unchecked Assumptions

The climate of a school improves in areas of motivation, learning, and cohesiveness if there is a concerted effort to reduce the number of unchecked assumptions among its leaders (Kaiser et al. 2012). Schools are social institutions where assumptions are made about students, parents, colleagues, and the administration. If these assumptions are inaccurate, what follows may distort people's thinking based on gossip, prejudice, and other forms of lateral violence. In order for critical thinking to take hold in schools, leaders may need to assess whether they are making unchecked assumptions about the everyday workings found in schools.

Here is one example of making an unchecked assumption. If a teacher sees a student in his or her classroom as a troublemaker, not based on behavior, but on being the brother of a troublemaking student from a previous year, the student may turn into a self-fulfilling prophecy and become a problem for the teacher and the school. Without taking the time to check out assumptions, school personnel suffer the reality of having to work with inaccurate information.

Here is one more example to make this point. A newly hired school principal tries to establish his or her authority by "making an example" of one teacher's negative behavior, assuming this will teach others a lesson if they misbehave. However, the climate of the school may suffer when teachers comply with the wishes of the school leader, while at the same time, having resentment toward such leadership.

Effective Leadership

In the case study, we saw many examples of school leaders working from unchecked assumptions. For example, leaders made the statement that in order to stop bullying in the school a zero-tolerance policy was required, even though it was proven not to work. Ironically, such an unchecked assumption increased punishments and rewards while further dividing the people in the school.

Here is another example. The leadership assumed increased bullying needs to be met with increased restrictions on the student body, even though increased restrictions on everyone did not reduce bullying in the school. What it created was the perception of leadership that practiced a similar type of reactionary behavior as the bullies. In a democratic form of school leadership, forceful action is viewed as a final option, not as a first reaction to such conflicts as bullying.

Clara treated bullying differently than school leaders. First, she was not in a position to change the school's reaction to bullying behavior. Instead, she concerned herself with operationally defining the goal of respect in her classroom. She wanted to check the assumption that more respect in the classroom would cause less reason for bullying behavior. In critically thinking through this problem, she included students, parents, and community members in the discussion. She created respect in the classroom by developing commitment displayed by others. She worked from assumptions based on the input of others, while critically thinking through ways to gain respect. Such concepts as respect, trust, and empowerment emerge by critically thinking through problems, rather than reacting to them.

Bias

Effective leaders broaden their perceptions of schools by becoming more democratic thinkers (Thiederman 2004). For example, when professionals in schools become self-centered or self-serving, biased thinking may tear down the positive elements found in the climate of schools. Leaders who only consider one aspect of a school problem can favor one group over another, while causing the school climate to deteriorate. For example, teachers who only reward high achievement in the classroom may devalue students with individual differences. Even if the teacher's intentions were not biased, the behavior of the teacher can be perceived as biased for those who respond to learning differently.

Critical thinking can relieve a school of subtle biases even when unintentional, while increasing a perception of fairness (Stanovich and West 2008). An example can be found in unbiased leaders who look at problems by considering their basic elements, but also the effects these problems have on the climate of the school. For example, school leaders who need to cut the school budget but do not consider the effects of such cuts on school morale, motivation, and the overall school environment have not critically thought through cutting the budget.

The leaders may end up being right and wrong at the same time. The budget cuts may be the right action to take, but how the budget was cut may infuriate other school personnel. Effective school leaders who believe and understand the value of critical thinking also believe in the dangers connected to bias, even unintentional bias.

Effective Leadership

In the case study, the school's zero-tolerance policy was not necessarily unwarranted. Many schools have zero-tolerance policies for weapons possession, drugs and alcohol abuse, cultural biases, sexual harassment, and bullying. What became questionable was the lack of critical thinking that went into implementing these policies. The bias of the school was in treating all bullying with suspension. When an outbreak of bullying took place in the school, the leadership showed their biases by punishing the entire school.

Unfortunately, the school's zero-tolerance response by its leaders lacked the tolerance needed for students to respect each other, another declared goal of the school. The connection between bullying and respect was not critically thought through. The school leaders demonstrated a bias toward valuing punishment over respect.

In more democratic forms of leadership, the "level of tolerance" becomes more important than the emphasis on zero-tolerance. In other words, different circumstances in schools require different responses. In the case study, there was little differentiation between bullies and their victims. The school believed such incidences disrupted the functioning of the school and suspended those involved in the incident. This behavior showed little critical thinking regarding the victims of bullying, and in this manner it revealed the leadership's bias toward punishment, rather than respect for the individual rights of students. It may surprise school leaders how clearly these subtle biases become obvious to other school personnel.

Facts and Opinions

So how do effective leaders in schools create a climate where critical thinking is an accepted practice? We have considered some of the groundwork for such thinking by not working from unchecked assumptions, and by considering broad perceptions when making decisions on school-related problems. Keeping this in mind, the difference between one-dimensional thinking and critical thinking may start with the leaders' ability to go beyond relying only on their personal facts and opinions (Almeida and Franco 2011).

How many schools activities are ruined by the tunnel vision of a teacher, counselor, or administrator who makes decisions based on a consideration of only one point of view? This is not to say one person's opinions are not important. However, school leaders acquire a better understanding of facts and opinions when considering many points of view.

Furthermore, certain decisions made by school leaders are based on opinions, especially opinions about how to maintain a healthy school climate. Effective leaders in schools look for opinions from many different sources in order to capture the essence of the facts (Murdach 2010). Being a critical thinker allows the school leader to comprehensively think through the facts related to any school-related problem. In order to effectively do that, leaders may need a wide variety of opinions from others.

How many problems are solved in schools by being an expert on the facts while coming to conclusions based on one-dimensional thinking? In some respects, being a one-dimensional expert can reduce critical thinking in schools. Multidimensional thinking through input from others not only makes thinking and deciding more factual, but it sets the tone for the type of thinking and decision making expected in the climate of a school.

Effective Leadership

In the case study, we see the difference between school leadership making faulty deductive assumptions and arguments based on zero-tolerance policies, while Clara made more effective inductive assumptions and arguments regarding the possible correlation between bullying and respect. An effective *deductive assumption* makes the claim that if the assumption is true then the argument is also true.

An effective *inductive assumption* makes the claim that if the assumption is true then the argument is not necessarily true, but it is a strong argument (Moore and Parker 2007). In the case study, the school leaders made the inaccurate deductive assumption that a zero-tolerance policy would reduce bullying and increase respect. Their assumption did not create a strong argument for having a zero-tolerance policy, at least their form of it.

On the other hand, Clara assumed that a connection existed between bullying and respect, and she proceeded to enact this assumption by working with students, parents, and the community. In the end, she could not claim that her assumption was true, but it seemed to have a strong probability for being accurate. Though Clara's actions in confronting the bullying and respect issue were not based on facts, they were acted out more successfully based on the critical thinking of those who gave input into the problem. Successful assumptions are based on doing something, and in having the critical-thinking skills to evaluate exactly what is being done.

Accuracy

Continuing from the section on facts and opinions, let us look at the accuracy of critical thinking in establishing a fair school climate for all, rather than an unfair climate that is beneficial for a chosen few. Being accurate in one's thinking takes place in schools when leaders compare different opinions and facts before making important decisions (Flemming 2010). For example, school leaders can write a new discipline policy by studying the research on effective discipline. In this case, accuracy is judged only on the efficacy of the research. Yet efficacy does not necessarily equal effectiveness in schools, where school climates have their individual differences. Democratic school leaders may look for accuracy by combining factual research with the opinions of others in the school.

Critical thinking in schools is as much about gathering accurate information that is proven effective, where facts and human experience are treated equally. A leader, who believes in democratic principles, may find this form of critical thinking a mandatory exercise. Systematically reflecting, in a fair-minded way, on accurate information through research and other means of obtaining facts and opinions is an important part of critical thinking in schools (Kalinowski 2010). Combining these facts with the opinions of others helps enhance the climate of a school. The skill of critical thinking becomes more accurate in schools when facts and opinions are considered along with how they impact on the climate of a school.

Effective Leadership

Leadership that think critically through problems find their accuracy in the reliability and validity established in the results. In the case study, there was little reliability or validity in the decision of school leaders to implement their version of a zero-tolerance policy for combating bullying and encouraging respect. In the end, neither goal was a reliable or valid representation of a successful program. At this point, it may be important to consider how accurate was Clara's attempt in confronting the same problem. She could not prove reliability or validity based on any statistical scale. Therefore, the efficacy of the results lacked statistical reliability and validity. However, statistical standards that apply to a research laboratory may be less important to a troubled school.

Using critical thinking to implement change in schools may be an opportunity for the use of qualitative research that is found in experiential learning (McClellan and Hyle 2012). Clara and others critically thought through the problem of respect by incorporating experiential activities in the classroom, and by doing this, she also addressed the bullying issue. The measure of its reliability and validity was based on its effectiveness when the school adopted these policies schoolwide. Accuracy in schools should be judged as much by a program's effectiveness as by its statistical efficacy.

Faulty Reasoning

Before continuing with our discussion on critical thinking, it may be important to clarify how faulty reasoning can create problems in a school climate:

- Critical thinkers usually check their assumptions about any given experience. Narrow-minded thinkers do not examine their assumptions.
- Critical thinkers have a broader perspective when solving problems. Narrow-minded thinkers can contaminate their thinking with biases.
- Critical thinkers make more calculated decisions based on facts and the opinions of others. Narrow-minded thinkers are random in their decisions.
- Critical thinkers act on problems. Narrow-minded thinkers react to problems.

Multidimensional thinking through input from others not only makes thinking and deciding more factual, but it sets the tone for the type of thinking and decision making expected in the school. When leaders critically think through a problem, their behavior becomes more proactive, creating a positive impact on schools. One of the problems facing a troubled school is when faulty reasoning by school leaders forms a foundation for reactionary behavior.

For example, school leaders may feel negative pressure from school personnel who are not responding favorably to their strict, authoritarian style of leadership. Such reactions by others may lead to faulty reasoning by leaders who assume they are "not strict enough." By not critically thinking through the problem, and by reacting negatively to criticism, school leaders may instigate further conflict in schools without even knowing it.

Once people in schools become aware of the faulty reasoning found in the reactionary behavior of school leaders, the chances for an escalation in conflict becomes a real concern. School personnel may shift, where they react according to their faulty reasoning, furthering the escalation of problems. Leaders practicing proactive behavior based on a fair, critical analysis of other people's thoughts and feelings can establish the practice of critical thinking, while tempering much of the faulty reasoning found in schools.

This may be why such programs as peer mediation in schools are successful (Cantrell, Parks-Savage, and Rehfuss 2007). These programs formally teach students to become critical thinkers by learning how to synthesize their thoughts and develop agreements based on proactive behavior.

Effective Leadership

In the case study, it may be difficult to determine which caused more conflict at Star Middle School: the bullying behavior of students, or the faulty reasoning of school leaders. Instead of being proactive, they overreacted with harsh punishment for everyone. They were trying to force the students into not being bullies. However, their faulty reasoning was in copying a similar form of force used by bullies to coerce their victims into submission. Their need to find blame and forcefully stop bullying behavior superseded their need to solve the bullying problem.

It may be important to point out that bullying at Star Middle School was not only a behavior problem. It also was a climate problem. The faulty reasoning of school leaders tried to solve one problem by creating another. In the case study, Clara believed changing the school's approach to bullying through input from families and community members would make it easier to face bullying behavior. Her reasoning was based on critically thinking through the whole problem more than in reacting to one part of it.

Judgments and Conclusions

School leaders who believe in the principles of democracy can influence a school climate by accurately judging the successes and failures of decisions made in schools. Not all activities in schools will have a positive outcome. A more democratic form of leadership relies on critical thinking to judge failure as well as success. In other words, critical thinkers learn from their mistakes (Shaker 2010). School leaders can improve the climate of a school by sharing conclusions regarding plans that did not work, or need revision. Making judgments and sharing conclusions, even negative conclusions, act as an opportunity for critical thinking by everyone involved.

A failed decision or project is not an evaluation of one's competence or ability to lead others. When looking at democratic leaders who have improved the climate of a school, one finds people who are making judgments and forming conclusions by proactively including others in the process, even in their failures (Bogotch 2010). Critical thinking is more about "How do we critically think through what has not worked?" as opposed to "Who is taking the blame for what has not worked?" Schools improve based on critically thinking together, rather than constant thoughts about individual successes or failures.

Effective Leadership

In the case study, Clara's leadership strength was in thinking through problems that did not work. She was not looking to blame bullies, their parents, or even the community for the negative school environment. She made judgments and conclusions by sharing the problem with others. She viewed respect as a moral value that could only be judged by those affected by a lack of it. She allowed for expressions of respect that were based on a common agreement. Yet she also let each individual apply his or her thoughts, but within the constraints of school policies and rules.

One of the tenets of a democratic leadership style is found in critical thinking, where judgments and conclusions are multidimensional, benefiting both the individual and the group. The adoption of Clara's policies school-wide emphasized the importance of dealing with a democratic approach to the problem of bullying. Instead of focusing on punishment for bullies and their victims, the emphasis was on respecting each other within the dimensions of a respectful school climate. She proved that critical thinking *can* work when problems are faced from a more multidimensional perspective.

SCHOOL VIOLENCE AND CRITICAL THINKING

Critical thinking may be the true enemy of school violence. People in schools who commit acts of violence have closed their minds to other options, where violence is not viewed as a problem, but as a solution to a problem—a solution that has eliminated other options. In contrast, critical thinking is an open-minded approach where a solution may change by thinking through a problem. In the case study, Clara analyzed what was needed to create respect in her classroom. She also acknowledged what she did not know, and spent time working with students, parents, and the community to learn more about respect and subsequently about bullying.

Such democratic procedures based on "critically thinking through problems" can have a surprisingly positive influence on a school. Schools that are clear in their structure and discipline, but also emphasize a school climate that provides a supportive connection with students, staff, and community, appear to have less violent crime and less bullying. A school leader that believes in democratic principles may consider the establishment of a climate based on critical thinking as a primary goal of leadership.

When you consider that 8 percent of students stay home from school because of bullying (Centers for Disease Control 2007), the importance of recognizing and responding to the potential of bullying in the climate of a school may be as critical as responding to bullying behavior. Most bullies do not see bullying as a problem but as a lifestyle; a lifestyle that may be imported into schools through association with peers, as in gangs, or through a family lifestyle, as in domestic violence (Blanchfield, Blanchfield, and Ladd 2008). Trying to change bullying behavior in schools without changing the lifestyle found in schools may result in temporary results, where the climate of a school tolerates these behaviors.

Programs that are based on a "whole school" approach seem more successful than approaches based only on changing behavior. In the case study, Clara took a whole-school approach that reduced violence in the school. She initiated critical thinking with all those affected by bullying. She took a proactive perspective, where changing to a more respectful lifestyle had an impact on the lifestyle of being a bully. In democratic schools, equal representation becomes a vital component of critical thinking skills, where all involved think through a problem. A school leader who establishes rules to combat violence but does not include those affected by the violence has not critically thought through school violence.

SUMMARY

In this chapter, we have explored how critical thinking is used to combat violence in schools. The emphasis was more on a proactive approach, where social and emotional strengths were emphasized over a reactive approach emphasizing zero-tolerance and punitive consequences. In the case study, Clara took a proactive approach by critically thinking through how to gain respect in her classroom. Yet her example can also stand for other issues in schools, such as empathy, resiliency, self-esteem, and academic success. More important was her emphasis on "connectedness" between peers, families, the school, and community (Smith and Sandhu 2004).

Clara was more preventive, solution driven, and holistic in her approach, all of which mark the signs of an effective critical thinker. She focused on social and emotional strengths, rather than on antisocial behavior. It may be that students who participate in nurturing and are supported and feel acceptance are better able to combat negative social behavior (Smith et al. 1996). Working from this assumption, the connection between school climate and violence can become as important as remedies for antisocial behavior in schools.

Effective school leaders need to ensure their assumptions include the climate of the school when facing violent behavior in schools. This may include a thorough understanding of the biases present in the school climate, and possibly within school leaders. This means that facts and opinions of others become a major ingredient when critically thinking through school problems, where a "whole school" approach may be a necessary prerequisite. This approach makes critically thinking through problems in schools more accurate, when all those affected by school violence are represented.

From a critical-thinking perspective, continually emphasizing antisocial, violent behavior instead of promoting democratic, prosocial behavior in schools seems to be the wrong approach. Approaches where constant intervention seem the norm creates a climate of intervention rather than a climate of prevention. Critical thinking in schools helps leaders to take a moment and slow down before reacting and to devise plans that systematically think through problems.

Chapter Ten

Generosity

The misconception by some is that generosity connected to schools is about giving money through philanthropy. Beyond philanthropy are more mindful definitions of generosity that are embraced by democratically oriented school leaders. For these professionals, generosity is more about giving freely, without judgment, and without a need of explanation. It is reaching an understanding about what it means to be helpful to others in a conscious and consistent manner. It includes improving the climate of the school that surrounds others and making their lives more meaningful. In this definition, generosity becomes about the ability to give freely of one's time and talents without special conditions of expecting something in return.

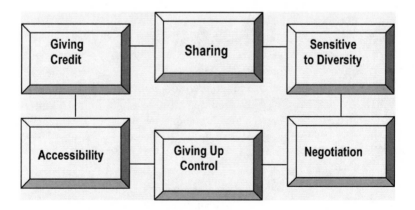

Figure 10.1.   An Outline for Generosity

For school leaders, generosity is the art of getting away from solely focusing on personal needs and recognizing the needs of others. In this chapter, generosity is explored through such themes as sharing with others, the importance of being sensitive to the diversity of others, how to negotiate with them, giving up a certain amount of control, and the importance of giving credit when credit is warranted.

These six principles do not exhaust the definition of generosity, but in the climate of a school, they go a long way in creating a more generous sense of sharing. In the contemporary atmosphere where achievement-based education can create a climate of greed (Karp 2008), generosity is the balance needed to make learning fair and productive, where healthy competition replaces focusing on one's personal needs over the needs of others.

CASE STUDY

Alexis was taking over for a dean of students who spent the past twenty-five years controlling student life at Brendle College, a small liberal arts college in the Northwest. The climate at Brendle was notoriously strained and student enrollments were dropping, primarily based on student reports to their parents. Apparently, the courses at the school were outstanding, but the climate in the dormitories was dreadful. Upon review of the student affairs handbook, Alexis wondered how any student could successfully leave the school with a positive attitude.

The handbook was mostly negative, based on what would happen to you if you broke the rules of student life. The former dean approached student life as though it was "boot camp," where rigorous discipline policies needed to be followed or operated under a three-strikes-and-out policy. This was implemented by resident directors writing up students for any indiscretions, where something similar to a "traffic ticket" was given, and where after three traffic tickets you were out.

The rumors and gossip about the dean and the resident directors filled the air of the dormitories each new semester. Apparently, the discipline code had become a conversation about who successfully graduated from the college and who did not, regardless of academic grade-point average. This was only complemented by the attitude of the student affairs staff who had taken on an insensitive, mean-spirited approach to students in the dorms. Students and student affairs administration seemed to be at odds, which only exacerbated dormitory drinking, smoking, and the use of drugs.

If it were not for the complaints from parents of Brendle students, the situation may have remained the same. However, Brendle was an alumni-supported college where alumni contributions were extremely important.

Since many of Brendle's students came from former alumni families, a switch had to be made.

This was the atmosphere facing Alexis when she took over the role as dean of students. When she had her first staff meeting, it came to her attention that she was meeting with people who were working from the assumptions previously held by the former dean. After her opening remarks, she asked her staff, "How many in this room have a fear of this coming semester being business as usual?" Slowly the hands were raised into the air until a few people expressed their fears. Her response was, "It has been reported to me that working here is an intimidating experience, but we are going to create a positive school climate together. We are going to help each other professionally, and at times, personally by turning the climate in the residence halls around."

For the next month, Alexis talked about the fear associated with working in student affairs. Alexis would match student affairs personnel with knowledgeable staff members in specific areas with new or uninformed staff members for information sharing. As it turned out, certain staff members were knowledgeable about the judicial policies and possible revisions to it, while others were sensitive to issues of diversity and the lack of sensitivity to people of color on the campus.

Alexis made the request that people get in groups and talk about topics that had little to do with student affairs but were important to them, such as having a social life, relationships, and other topics. The discussions continued until plans for change began emerging from the meetings. What developed were negotiated changes to improve the climate of student life on campus.

During these meetings, Alexis would sit in on different groups more as a resource person than as a leader. She gave over control to facilitators who gathered information after the meetings and formalized plans that were presented to the administration of the college. In the end, some of the policies were changed, such as having a formal mediation program as a part of the judicial process and establishing a general space in one of the dormitory lounges for expressions of diversity through workshops, art exhibits, and luncheons.

But most policies were only changed regarding implementation: students still had to adhere to drug and alcohol policies, yet counseling and mentoring was provided for those who drifted away from following them. Instead of the emotional climate of student affairs remaining punitive, it had taken on a different attitude, one of generosity and fairness. Furthermore, those students who initiated change were recognized by the school for their commitment to change and were honored by Alexis at college functions and during convocation and commencement. With time, Brendle College had regained its reputation not only for academic rigor but also for being a school where generosity became a part of college education.

GENEROSITY AND SCHOOL CLIMATE

Sharing

In order for effective leaders in schools to begin a process of generosity, they must make an assumption that getting involved with others is not only important, but becomes a school-oriented goal (Lloyd-Smith and Baron 2010). Leaders who want a peaceful environment in schools create methods and activities for others to share in their goals and aspirations. For example, a school leader who shares the responsibility of setting guidelines for school discipline, not only with other staff but also with parents and students, may be in a better position to enforce those guidelines. One of the more serious mistakes made by school leaders is to rigidly structure the guidelines of schools without other people's involvement.

Setting up school rules on one's own may be more efficient in the development of these rules. However, even if that is correct, it does not mean that sharing with others is unnecessary. By involving others, school leaders not only allow for other points of view, but they also allow for generosity to form within groups. Students, staff, and parents know of those leaders who keep things to themselves, sending a message to school personnel that "I am in charge and we will be doing things my way." This message may be more important to others than whatever guidelines or activities these leaders are trying to accomplish. It may be their lack of sharing is taken as self-centered or greedy, when it takes little extra effort to include others in the process, even when only as a formality (Kanngiesser, Warneken, and Young 2012).

Effective Leadership

In the case study, Alexis included other staff members in the reconstruction of the student affairs program at Brendle College, and it was not a formality. Sometimes, leadership can confuse being an expert with the artistry that goes into sharing goals and responsibilities with others. The art of sharing is a fundamental ingredient in being a democratic leader in schools that can directly have an impact on the climate of a school. It is a part of the hidden curriculum for success when working with intelligent professionals with insightful and valid points of view. In the case study, Alexis shared problems with her staff that were causing a negative effect on the school's enrollment. However, she did not force her staff to share, but encouraged sharing in small groups.

Here is another part of sharing that can be overlooked by school leadership. No one should force others to share. In the case study, forcing others to share would be as unproductive as the former dean of students forcing others to follow the rules. True sharing is based on generosity, not on compliance. The effective use of sharing bolsters interpersonal relationships between people. In the case study, Alexis was as interested in formulating stronger interpersonal relationships as she was in solving the problems of student affairs. She understood that both were intricately connected.

How many school leaders miss the connection between solving school problems and establishing interpersonal relationships? School leaders who understand the tenets of generosity have a stronger chance of connecting sharing, interpersonal relationships, and solving school problems, all being vital ingredients in dealing with conflict in schools.

Sensitive to Diversity

Practicing generosity in schools may need democratic leaders who focus on more than just procedural goals such as curriculum, budget, and rules enforcement. These leaders may need to consider more *affective goals* such as being sensitive to the diverse needs of others (Dierdorff, Surface, and Brown 2010). When other people perceive leaders as sensitive to their needs, a sense of generosity continues to develop. Professionals in the field of conflict resolution understand that sensitivity to others means you have taken the time in your day to *be with others.*

This becomes a vital consideration in today's multicultural environment, where having an understanding of diversity requires more than an awareness of diversity. Generosity in today's schools requires school leaders to immerse themselves in the subcultures of those in the climate of schools. You can work together, but that does not guarantee you can *be together.* Sometimes leaders become myopic in their vision of schools. They see areas that need attention according to the guidelines found in their job descriptions. They may even be highly effective in their roles. That does not mean they will be effective with others.

Democratic school leaders may need sensitivity to individual differences in those who follow the mandates and guidelines found in schools (Starr 2010). In today's schools, having little awareness of diversity may change other people's views of the leader's role. In a more authoritarian leadership style, insensitivity to the diverse needs of others and focusing obsessively on goals sometimes sabotages the hard work put into the guidelines of a job description.

Others observing such leaders may receive a different message beyond what is being conveyed through guidelines and rules. They may perceive that these leaders are being self-centered and self-serving, rather than hard working or following guidelines necessary for running a school. They may see leaders who are insensitive and do not recognize their diversity by sending a subtle message that differences hold little value.

Effective Leadership

In the case study, Alexis understood the importance of immersing herself in the diverse roles and backgrounds of her staff. She had the wisdom to create a "public space" in one of the dormitory lounges for expressions of diversity. Here we see an example of a leader who integrated generosity with diversity by creating a multicultural environment for those affected by the rules and guidelines of the school. Through her efforts, Alexis made the statement, "You can be different yet be a part of the whole." She found the common ground needed to "be with" a diverse staff of people who had the responsibility for creating a more diverse student body.

It may be the responsibility of school leaders to create a shared sense of "public space" or common space where diversity can flourish beyond each person's individual space. How many seeds of violence are planted when someone in the school feels there is no place to practice their diversity, no shared sense of space or common ground? How many violent acts can be averted if the people in charge show generosity with their time and recognize the need for sharing space with others?

In achievement-based schools, where success and making the grade seem paramount, the seeds of resentment and anger can develop for those who feel unnoticed and outside the circle of the school. The practice of being sensitive to the needs of others can create an unspoken rule that generosity is a vital component within diverse groups pursuing a common goal. Over time, generosity encourages faculty and staff to reach out and help others and to feel within the circle of learning and not on its fringes.

Negotiation

In conflict resolution, the statement, "You cannot get water from an empty bucket" may apply to this stage of generosity and leadership within schools. The question continuously asked when violence erupts in schools is, "Why did he or she who appeared nonviolent suddenly become violent?" One reason may be that school personnel do not help fill that person's "bucket," or they do not recognize that it is empty. Learning conflict resolution and communication skills may be a necessary requirement if leaders value generosity in schools (Gardner 2005).

In the field of conflict resolution, an agreement where one party gets all needs met, but the other party gets none of their needs met would be considered an ineffective agreement. Sometimes, it appears to faculty and staff that leaders continually ask for more to be done yet receive little in return. Generosity is felt when something meaningful is being negotiated. It is when leaders solve problems with others, and share credit for the results.

Generosity may be about school leaders using their power to negotiate win-win situations. School leaders go a long way in having the needs of the school met by simply negotiating with the staff. This can be anywhere from simply checking in to a full participation in a project. People are willing to negotiate when the leadership seems interested in their input (Page and Mukherjee 2009). Furthermore, negotiation helps with two different goals. It can obtain valuable input from others that may help strengthen the goals of a leader, and it "fills the bucket" of the staff where, in the future, they may have something to negotiate.

Effective Leadership

In the case study, much of Alexis's style surrounded the skills of negotiation. She constantly worked for the common ground between differing points of view. She broke into groups and eventually established policies based on negotiation such as a formal mediation program. Generosity in schools is as much about disagreement as it is about agreement. This democratic principle seems filled with a sense of generosity. It makes the statement that leaders are willing to share and be sensitive to diverse points of view through the process of negotiation.

The message sent to others is that the most cherished and long-standing rules and guidelines in any institution can stand the test of a reasonable negotiation. In the case study, Alexis negotiated much of the rules governing student affairs. Ironically, very little changed regarding these rules, except for some additions such as mediation. What did change was the college's willingness to include others in negotiation of these rules and guidelines. Generosity was further established by having such a discussion, even if little changed regarding the school's rules and guidelines.

Giving Up Control

Many school leaders do not understand the paradox found in giving control over to others. Helping to create generosity in schools by giving over partial control to others allows school leaders to maintain control in schools. The paradox is that the more leaders give up some form of control in schools, the more they maintain control in the form of support (Moye and Langfred 2004). Giving up control in schools is different than giving away a physical object. When a person gives control to others, it can create a sense of generosity in others.

It could be said that holding tight control over schools could contribute to a climate of potential violence. When leaders in schools stop being generous, and school personnel become polarized, then conflict and possibly violence seem possible. Control truly is a paradox: the more you give away the more you get in return. Those leaders looking for generosity from parents, staff, and students may need an understanding of this paradox if they expect others to participate in sharing the goals and aspirations found in schools. Giving over partial control in schools can establish a strong sense of common ground, and schools that have a sense of common ground may have less possibility for school violence (Bryan and Lynette 2012).

Effective Leadership

In the case study, Alexis had an understanding of this principle. She gave partial control over to her staff, thus combining generosity with empowerment. For more democratic leaders, the art of humanizing a school requires both empowerment and generosity. In the case study, Alexis combined empowerment with generosity in order to create a sense of freedom. These elements were denied in the previously oppressive administration of the former dean of students, where keeping power and control was conveyed to everyone involved as the major issue of importance.

Sometimes, what people say is not necessarily what they mean. The former dean of students made statements about the importance of controlling the climate at Brendle College. However, what was conveyed to others was, "I am in control!" Here we see a statement based on forcing one's will on others rather than one that tries to create a climate that was under control. On the other hand, Alexis created an environment that was under control by partially giving up control through generosity and empowerment.

Accessibility

The people within a school may find it difficult to share if school leaders are not accessible to letting them share. The concept of accessibility is a subtle one. This not only means the leader's door is always open (though probably that is an important concept to keep in mind). It also means the leader's mind is always open. Here are considerations that go beyond being geographically available. These considerations include (1) a sense of sharing, (2) sensitivity to diversity, (3) giving over partial control, and (4) being physically and emotionally accessible, which is all a part of successful social networking in institutions (Chrispeels 2004).

School leadership may require accessible network connections with faculty, students, and parents on many issues involving the effective functioning of schools. Such leaders are not afraid to share their opinions, and should remain accessible for others' opinions through creating effective social networks.

Democratic leadership may have a responsibility in creating social networks where people become sensitive to each other. When this happens, generosity stops being a cliché, a high-level abstraction. Generosity becomes a practical matter, where leaders network with others in making schools more productive places to learn, while being safer places to work. The seeds of violence do not come from generosity, and they are more likely to appear in schools as a result of greed. A climate of greed is built on secrecy, where people feel justified in hurting others and where insensitivity and obsession replace negotiation, sharing, and accessibility, all key ingredients in social networking.

Effective Leadership

In the case study, social networking with staff was a major goal when Alexis became dean of students. She understood that the seeds of democracy are planted with the ability of people to be accessible to each other. However, this may bring up a comparison between accessibility and privacy with the influx of social networking. The case study does not include current social networking such as Facebook and Twitter, yet it seems feasible that these network devices could be used as a means for creating accessibility in schools. But as in all forms of communication, the formation of guidelines may need consideration.

In the case study, Alexis could set up guidelines for social networking between parents, students, administration, and professors, as long as abuses found in such networks were taken into consideration, especially issues of privacy. Cyberbullying is one aspect of social networking getting a lot of attention, where abusing accessibility does not lead to democracy but to oppression. Privacy with accessibility is as big a concern when creating a climate of generosity in schools.

Giving Credit

Are we living in an age of greed, where it is all about ourselves and not about the group? Whether the answer to this question is true or not can be debated. In considering the climate of a school, it may be important to give credit where credit is due, and not take credit for those areas that should not have our names on them. Effective school leaders wanting to create generosity understand the importance of giving credit to an individual or group (Angelle 2007). Creatomg a climate where people give credit to others demonstrates the success of establishing generosity within a school. Effective leaders know how to promote the accomplishments of individuals in schools instead of simply promoting winners and losers.

Acts of generosity through giving credit can expand the reasons for credit. A leader may consider going beyond giving credit for achievement. (It may be giving credit for achievement is more of a reward than an honor.) This has become the stereotypical reason for giving credit. With generosity, a leader can give credit in other areas where people are honored, not only rewarded.

For example, helping others in a time of need, or being the person who helped to motivate working on a project, are not necessarily about getting a reward, but they are honorable and important to the climate of a school. Giving this type of credit to others gets people involved, where generosity can continue to grow.

Effective Leadership

In the case study, Alexis did not miss this point in her pursuit of generosity with the student affairs program. She made sure that formal recognition went to members of her staff during critical moments in the school's experience, such as when she honored her staff both at convocation and commencement. However, honoring someone or giving them credit is different than rewarding them. Giving someone credit is based on appreciation for the hard work they have contributed to meeting a common goal.

Rewarding someone is based on giving privileges for following the basic guidelines or rules. With generosity, people honor each other rather than give rewards. Giving credit for a job well done is more of an honor than a reward. Practicing generosity in a democratic style of leadership is more about honoring people than in giving rewards for doing what you are told.

Constantly giving rewards to certain people in schools for doing what they are told can, in certain circumstances, polarize a group. For example, when the same students in public schools are constantly rewarded for their academic achievement at such activities as graduation ceremonies, the message conveyed to others is that the same people are always the ones rewarded for what they can achieve. However, with generosity, such rewards are valuable as long as they are balanced with honoring others for *who they are* in the climate of a school, beyond being rewarded for achievement. Generosity in schools is as much about recognizing honorable people as in rewarding a select few for some form of accomplishment.

SCHOOL VIOLENCE AND GENEROSITY

Creating nonviolent schools based on the principle of generosity may require its leaders to reach out and share the problem of violence through community-wide collaborative efforts that include students, teachers, staff, families, mental health professionals, emergency response personnel, law enforcement, and the business community. However, violence addressed in this chapter focused more on "invisible violence." These are the subtle activities that take place every day that send the message, "I am in charge," and "I am thinking only of myself."

In the case study, this was the subtle message of violence sent by the former dean of students. It was a message that created a dangerous set of unspoken rules, namely, "The rules at the college are meant to oppress you, not protect you," and "You have little input in changing these rules." Conversely, Alexis changed these unspoken rules to "We are in charge" and "We are thinking of each other." In a subtle, yet critical manner, the rules of the college began a shift, namely, "The rules of the college will include you" and "You have input into changing these rules."

It may be the subtleties found in everyday human interaction in schools that plant seeds of violence, along with negative life events. Working from this assumption, creating a climate of generosity can reduce the seeds of violence while planting a sense of sharing, negotiating, and giving up partial control. Such principles reflect a more democratic form of leadership where generosity is not simply an act of altruism, but a practical method for controlling violence in schools. The Bath School Disaster, Virginia Tech Massacre, and University of Texas Massacre are some of the most infamous incidents of school violence where generosity may have influenced different outcomes (Johnson 2009).

All of these examples have characteristics based on psychological problems of the predators involved in these incidences, but they also have evidence reflecting how they were treated socially in the climate found in their respective schools (Ludwig and Warren 2009). Generosity as a combatant to school violence has little research evidence, at this time, to support its effect on school violence. However, common sense tells us that people feeling a part of an organization, having a sense of empowerment in it, having access to the leaders of the organization, and receiving credit for a commitment to the organization may be less likely to commit a violent act against that organization.

SUMMARY

This chapter combined the concepts of sharing with diversity found in human experience. It further added the purpose behind negotiation, and giving over control in schools. It showed the value in being accessible, along with the importance of giving credit. In all of these themes, the experience of generosity revealed its importance in creating a democratic leadership style in schools. It described leaders who are not solely focused on their job descriptions, but include others in these descriptions. Through generosity, democratic leaders in schools can make their impact on the climate of a school.

Though it may sound risky, such generosity can become more important in violence-oriented schools. Keeping control and limiting moments of generosity may appear on the surface as less risky, yet it may increase the risk of violence in schools. Confusing generosity with a lack of safety can be a mistake. Schools can practice the tenets of generosity found in this chapter and still maintain a climate of safety. School leaders, trying to constantly keep a school safe, may be less effective than sharing that responsibility with others who have an equal investment in school safety.

Terms such as *sharing, giving over power, accessibility, giving credit,* and *negotiating* with others can be misconstrued to mean letting down one's guard. Yet in democratic schools, accomplishing the goal of generosity may help everyone in the school make an effort in keeping the school a safer place to learn and develop. In this regard, generosity goes beyond being an altruistic virtue to be followed, and becomes a practical method of leadership, where sharing the whole becomes stronger than the sum of its parts.

Chapter Eleven

Trust

Trust may be the glue needed by school leaders that keeps interpersonal relationships cohesive and alive. Trust works best when people in schools understand what is expected of them, and have a clear understanding of what is expected of others (Comer et al. 1996). This chapter explores the tenets involved in creating trust in the climate of a school, from initially reaching out to others to the end result of developing professional loyalties. It also will explore how people in schools depend on each other, especially when feeling mutually vulnerable in situations where direct or indirect violence take hold of a school climate. It may be when school leaders take personal action in reducing a sense of vulnerability in others that helps build trust across a school community.

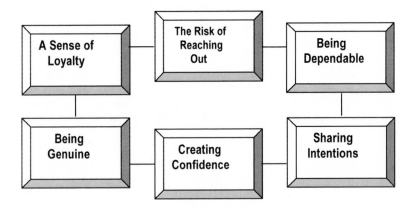

Figure 11.1.   An Outline for Trust

In order to create trust, it becomes important for school leaders to make their intentions known (Waldron, McLeskey, and Redd 2011). Beyond what people say to each other in schools are the intentions behind what is said. When school leaders talk to school personnel, questions are raised in their minds, for example, "How do the leader's statements affect my self-esteem?" or "How do the leader's statements advance my self-interests?"

This becomes important within a school climate where trust is well established and such questions are more clearly understood. When school leaders initiate changes within a school, trust can be a mandatory ingredient. Trust creates the confidence needed and reduces the sense of risk when making change. When people in schools trust their leaders, they feel safer when experimenting with new practices (Daly and Chrispeels 2008).

Trust in schools also may be a collection of simple interactions based on genuinity and the expression of positive regard. Simple interactions can lead to more complex interactions, where trusting each other and making change in schools have a reciprocal relationship. A school leader's ability to consistently act with integrity on a day-to-day basis when addressing school affairs allows for the creation of trust within the climate of a school.

Leadership in schools requires effective management of curriculum, budgets, rules, and guidelines, but without trust these administrative duties take on a complicated reality, especially when school personnel are asked to participate in directives they may not completely understand (Kutsyuruba, Walker, and Noonan 2011). In such circumstances, trust becomes a vital ingredient in maintaining a healthy school climate.

CASE STUDY

Dorian had turned the school district around. The district was burdened with violence, bad relations between the school and the community, and by a staff that felt deceived by the previous administrator. However, all of that had changed, as he remembered those first days after taking over as the district superintendent. It was a time filled with cautious behavior from the school and the community. Violence plagued the school through bullying behavior and in the community, with drive-by shootings directed at a few of the school's top students. It was obvious to Dorian that the school district was not conducive to a climate of trust. Different groups within the school were working as independent contractors, not supporting or connected to each other.

Beyond the organization of the school was student life, which worked against trust by grouping students along the lines of social class and race. Furthermore, the school schedule moved at lightning speed, not allowing time to build trust, or even have a meaningful conversation about it. The district was constantly on edge, and this was reflected in its students.

Parents complained to Dorian about how their children were living in fear from dangers residing in the community and were also afraid to make mistakes in school, which only added to their fear. This was not hard to believe, based on teachers demonstrating similar behavior toward Dorian. Achievement was their top priority, yet teachers felt skeptical whether the school district knew how to effectively accomplish this goal.

Yet Dorian had turned the school district around. Was it his plans for a new curriculum or discipline code, or did he have a research base model that improved school efficiency? It was none of these. He based improvements in the school district mostly on creating a climate of trust. This was his goal, and he decided to hold off on other plans until his goal was reached.

His first activity was to reach out to parents, community members, teachers, and students. He held meetings with all of these groups, but instead of presenting his plans for change, he simply listened to them. He first wanted to know them professionally and personally, and he met with different groups until they were comfortable with each other.

In one group, he listened to parents and how gangs had infiltrated the community and how the lack of response from the former superintendent alienated community members from participating in school-based activities. In another group, he heard how certain students acted as bullies, demanding money or threatening others to suffer the consequences. He talked to teachers, who complained of the pressures put on them, and how they wished the stressful atmosphere in the school would go away.

Dorian listened, and slowly people began to depend on him to follow through on their concerns. He accomplished this by *not* making major changes in, for example, school discipline, but minor acknowledgments through giving feedback. He also tried doing any number of attempts to change these situations. What they seemed to like about him was how he kept them informed. Dorian made small changes such as longer lunch periods, and larger changes, as in considering a more multicultural curriculum for the school district.

Dorian sought out agreement from them, but welcomed disagreement. People connected to the school district slowly began feeling confident. They could agree to disagree, but regardless, "Dorian would talk to you." What they liked about Dorian was that "he said was what he meant." He was not a school leader sending mixed messages, but he was clear, specific, and real, and the school began to appreciate this style of leadership, even during difficult times.

Over time, Dorian did turn the school district around. There were difficult times, yet they seemed safer and less threatening when being addressed by their school superintendent. Dorian created a sense of loyalty in his faculty and staff based on human characteristics such as being genuine and dependable, and a willingness to take risks. His behavior encouraged others to practice similar patterns of behavior.

Dorian became more than an effective administrator. He became a role model for others to follow. When changing the school, he did not conceive major plans for change but practiced the principles needed in creating a trusting school climate. Dorian worked from the assumption that "if people trust you, then they will make the school district a better place to live and learn."

TRUST AND SCHOOL CLIMATE

The Risk of Reaching Out

Leaders who are interested in creating trust may need to take risks, if trust is lacking in a school. Trust begins by reaching out to others and engaging them in an authentic manner. There is a saying, "There is doing the smart thing and doing the right thing, and trust develops when the smart thing and the right thing are the same thing." There are leaders who try to "play to the crowd," and only reach out toward others when it benefits them. They may believe this is the smart thing to do, but is it the right thing? Trust begins in schools when people begin to reach out to others because their conscience compels them to do the "right thing."

For example, school personnel who are struggling with a dispute may trust a leader who reaches out and offers to help them, rather than the leader making a judgment about their dispute (Kutsyuruba, Walker, and Noonan 2011). The seeds of trust are planted in such an exchange where the leader is reaching out for the common good, and offers help beyond making judgments based on right or wrong.

Effective Leadership

Trust begins by taking a risk and reaching out. School leaders can develop trust by setting examples based on reaching out and risking for the common good. In the case study, Dorian reached out for the common good. He had no specific plan to change the climate of the school. He risked by reaching out and listening. In this sense, he based trust on the courage involved in taking a risk. How many school leaders do you know who avoid risk while sitting in judgment of others? When leaders reach out, the message sent is this: "We are willing to risk personal involvement for the common good of everyone involved." Such leaders gain trust when they are the first to reach out and take risks in the school environment.

Being Dependable

If you are going to reach out to help others, then it becomes imperative that others can depend on you for help. Some school leaders say, for example, "My door is always open," only to find the door closed most of the time. Trust begins by the risk involved in reaching out to others and is maintained when others realize the leader is dependable (Chhuon et al. 2008). You may know of leaders who are friendly, warm, and get along with their staff, but when it is time to follow through on a difficult task, somehow these leaders are not present, or fail to support the task at hand.

Being a dependable leader is partially based on having a sense of commitment to others. For example, a school leader may acknowledge the needs of others as important, yet acknowledgment requires little risk. How many sympathetic leaders have acknowledged the problems facing a school, but do little in following through to address these problems?

Effective Leadership

Developing trust in leadership requires a certain dedication to following through that allows others to recognize the leadership as dependable. In other words, dependable leaders make a commitment to others and will "come through" when needed. Coming through or following through when others are in need is by definition an act of dependability. In the case study, Dorian was able to follow through on what others were telling him, even in the smallest ways. He was committed to those in the school, not only when situations were positive, but also when they fell short of being that way.

Dependable leaders act as a safety net for others by breaking their fall or by buffering their pain. A lack of dependability can do the opposite, where distrustful school leaders may help in justifying frustration and indirect forms of violence. People in schools trust those people they can depend on to follow through, and they begin to distrust those that cannot.

Sharing Intentions

Reaching out and being dependable becomes solidified when leaders consistently share their intentions with others. This may be a controversial issue for some, based on whether one believes other people can handle the leader's intentions in a school. For some school leaders, knowledge sharing seems a risky business. The issue of sharing intentions may involve whether school leaders are open to others witnessing their intentions and whether the beliefs of leaders match their behavior. Distrust can take hold in a school when leaders openly smile at the faces of others, assuring that nothing has changed, while deceptively changing policies and procedures in a school.

For example, if leaders know that job cuts are forthcoming in a school, is it wise to hold out on the intentions of leadership, or do leaders take the risk of self-disclosure? In this case, sharing intentions in order to maintain trust may be a matter of timing more than intentions. A leader may disclose that job cuts are forthcoming, and as the date draws closer they give periodic announcements in preparation for such a traumatic event. Sharing intentions may be more about timing than in making the assumption: "People in the school will not be able to handle my intentions."

Effective Leadership

Trust in schools is based more on other people's perceptions of its leaders taking the risk of sharing their intentions. They may expect leaders to consistently share their intentions, even when the information conveyed is negative. If school leaders have effectively shared their intentions in the past, then the expectation of others may be they will share their intentions in the present.

In the case study, this was the style of leadership that Dorian practiced as superintendent of schools. He shared his intentions after listening to the intentions of others. In order to trust in one's leadership, it may be important to differentiate the sharing of intentions from how intentions are shared with others. People may be willing to trust the intentions of leaders if they first listen to others, and then present their intentions in a respectful and timely manner.

Creating Confidence

If leaders reach out, act in a dependable manner, and share intentions, these actions may be the seeds for creating confidence in school leaders, while creating confidence in schools. When people feel confident they may associate it with feeling safe, motivated, and without a sense of fear (Hofkins 2010). However, having confidence in leaders is something that must be earned. For example, some school leaders may act confident in order to hide their insecurities and inadequacies. False confidence kills a sense of trust in schools. Sometimes such leaders are strict and use force to prove their confidence.

In the end, creating confidence in schools is less about making a confident impression on others, and more about feeling safe, motivated, and less fearful when teaching, counseling, or coaching. Confidence levels may begin to deteriorate when leaders do not reach out, do not act in a dependable manner, and do not share their intentions. These leaders kill confidence even in the most confident situations. Creating confidence can also attest to other leadership skills such as humor, empowerment, and assertiveness. Confidence is a frame of mind, where leaders and staff trust each other and are confident of that trust (Rashid and Edmondson 2012).

Effective Leadership

In the case study, Dorian understood the difference between true confidence and a false sense of confidence. A false sense of confidence is based on the insecurity of *needing to be right* as opposed to *wanting to be right* (Ladd 2009). Usually leaders with a false sense of confidence act as if they know more than others, or have a more sophisticated expertise, in order to prove their confidence. In the case study, Dorian had nothing to prove. He confidently opened up discussions with many different groups, simply to listen to them. He worked from a sense of confidence that if he listened closely, and helped when he could, then the school would begin to improve.

Leaders such as Dorian can improve the confidence of others by taking this attitude. Instead of condescending through a false sense of confidence, school leaders can open up to others and ask for their help and for their sense of confidence. Confidence in schools can be a reciprocal relationship between the help given between school leaders and other school personnel. In the case study, the school district gained confidence in itself through this reciprocal relationship.

Being Genuine

School leaders who reach out and risk, as opposed to how others depend on people to share their intentions, create a sense of confidence in one's leadership, and this can make the school a place where honesty and genuineness are highly regarded. Trust can be contagious in schools, and by being a school leader who is considered genuine, dependable, and confident, it allows others to model similar behavior (Rogers 1983). In the climate of a school, the more others view leaders as genuine, the more possibility for others to be genuine.

Creating genuineness in schools is based on creating momentum for all involved to tell the truth, as they know it. When people start acting in this manner, interactions filled with genuineness can test those traumatic times when direct and indirect violence become a part of the landscape of the school. Genuineness in schools counteracts issues directed toward lateral violence such as gossiping, ambushing, and sabotage. Even if these still happen, others may perceive the school as a place where genuineness will prevail over deception, and where possible violence is thwarted by trust.

Effective Leadership

A lack of genuineness can create subtle forms of violence in schools. When school personnel are under the impression that school leaders are not being authentic and genuine, this sends a message that deception is a part of the unspoken rules of a school. Anger, resentment, jealousy, and possibly revenge can become issues when school personnel believe the administration is deceptive. Trust then takes a back seat to lateral violence, where gossiping and passive-aggressive behavior have an opportunity to set the tone for the entire school (Ladd and Churchill 2012).

Genuineness helps clarify the unspoken rules of a school by consistently having people's behavior match their intentions. In this manner, schools remain places where clear communication is valued, and where deception is counteracted by authenticity. In the case study, Dorian demonstrated the power of genuineness. By constantly checking in with others and by telling them the truth as he knew it, they began seeing him as an authentic, genuine person, not only as the school superintendent. His genuineness set the tone for the development of unspoken rules where others could be genuine. He added a sense of authenticity to the school climate.

A Sense of Loyalty

Loyalty seems to be the end result of creating trust in schools. School personnel, having experienced a leader who is risk taking, dependable, confident, and genuine, are more likely to be loyal to the leader and the school. Loyalty to leaders and schools is about making a personal investment, and taking partial ownership in the ideas, beliefs, and practices of these leaders and their schools (Hoy and Rees 1974). Loyalty may be the guiding force in schools, even when others disagree with their leaders.

For example, when a situation arises in which a decision made by a leader appears to hurt the school, yet the leader states, "Trust me, it will be alright": If trust is intact, people may suspend judgment, hold off action, and wait for the leader to come through. Such behaviors denote a certain level of loyalty toward that leader. Many of us understand deception, violence, and manipulation, and we may be aware when they are happening in a school. Yet loyalty toward school leadership may give a leader the flexibility needed in moving the school away from such experiences.

Effective Leadership

For some, loyalty may be described as a high-level ideal, or something that is more philosophical rather than realistic, especially regarding violence in schools. In essence, loyalty seems a practical part of keeping violence out of schools. For example, we may make a comparison with violent gangs that try to infiltrate a school. Many of them gain their strength through forced loyalty to the gang leader. This unhealthy expression of loyalty in a school can be counteracted with a genuine sense of loyalty.

For example, in the case study, one of the problems facing the school district was the behavior of violent gangs. However, Dorian created a true sense of loyalty in the faculty, students, and their parents. School leaders can gain strength when loyal school personnel come together to counteract violence in schools. Loyalty is an investment, whether it is a gang or a school. A school climate based on trust may need an investment through expressions of loyalty in order to gain the strength needed in facing school-related violence.

SCHOOL VIOLENCE AND TRUST

Most students do not practice violent acts in schools. Nor do they carry guns or knives; nor are they members of gangs. Yet common forms of violence do happen in schools, usually in the form of physical and emotional abuse. In the case study, gang violence was an issue but also was bullying. Name calling, threatening, and putting another person down, along with hitting, punching, and shoving, are more likely to be directly connected to a climate of trust than whether outside acts of violence indirectly influence a school (Johnson et al. 2012). It is this type of violence in schools that violates trust, and diminishes school efforts in educating students.

Research clearly shows that victims of school violence are at increased risk of social, emotional, and academic problems (Jimerson et al. 2006). In the case study, Dorian promoted nonviolence in the school, not by any major program to address violence. He did not directly address specific violent behaviors, but he altered the school climate by creating a sense of trust among school personnel. He was more concerned with people being connected to the school than any specific program. It was his acts of creating connectedness that developed trust among teachers, parents, students, and the community.

Yet this leads to an essential dilemma in some schools. It is hard to argue that safety precautions should be enforced for those few percent that can bring violence into schools. Metal detectors, body searches, and zero-tolerance policies fall under the argument, "Why take a chance?" Gun violence is a reality, but also is the fear that may be generated by such safety-oriented procedures. It may be that a balanced approach is needed, especially for those democratic school leaders who also value creating trust in schools.

An overemphasis on safety may inhibit establishing a climate of trust. The threat of violence may diminish when school leaders who reach out and risk are seen as dependable and genuine, and they create confidence in others who are loyal to that leader. Creating trust may be as important as controlling a fear of violence. For democratic school leaders who believe in the power of trust, creating this balance between safety and trust may be a defining issue in what type of school climate prevails.

In the case study, Dorian chose to focus on creating a climate of trust, rather than emphasizing the gang incidences or the bullying in the school district. He chose to listen while remaining genuine and dependable. With time, he created a sense of loyalty in the participants of the school. Controlling violence in schools is as much about balancing trust in a school with one's fear of violence through direct actions, such as metal detectors, locker searches, and zero-tolerance policies.

Loyalty to a school leader may be as important in confronting school violence as safety procedures. Through trust, violence can be prevented in schools, such as bullying and other indirect forms of violence. For the small percentage of violence brought into schools, moderation should be considered when using safety devices and procedures to protect school personnel. A small percentage of school-related violence coming into a school should not be a reason for focusing primarily on safety over trust.

SUMMARY

This chapter demonstrated the importance of trust in establishing an effective school climate. Trust includes the courage of school leaders to reach out and connect with others. This requires personal risk that may go beyond the leadership job description. Yet without risk, the possibility of others feeling safe may be diminished. In the case study, we saw a leader who was willing to take a personal risk and listen to others. Such vulnerability may send a message to school personnel that "we are in this together. Let us work together in making this school a better place for everyone."

However, simply reaching out may not change another's perceptions unless school leaders consistently reach out. Under these conditions, school personnel, parents, students, and the community gain a sense of dependability in such leaders. It also becomes important in creating trust that leaders remain clear about their intentions. Hidden agendas that surprise school personnel may be valid changes in a school, but others may focus more on the surprise than on change. In a climate of trust, letting others know one's intentions serves as an invitation into the "thinking of a leader," leading to partial ownership of what the leader is thinking.

Such ownership may be the confidence school personnel need to trust the actions of its leaders. Confidence in schools does not come from deceptive practices, but from shared intentions. Establishing a sense of confidence in a school climate makes schools more genuine places to work, where what people say is what they mean. Mixed messages in schools may lead more toward indirect violence, while genuine messages can add to school confidence.

In the end, trust includes all of the above factors leading to a sense of loyalty in schools. Loyalty can influence the climate of a school, where school personnel trust that its leaders will follow through. Found within a school climate without trust and loyalty are school personnel with divided loyalties, to one's self or to a select few. Democratic school leaders believing in the power of trust also invest in the power of school loyalty.

It has been addressed in earlier chapters that issues of school violence can adopt the proper safety procedures in schools. However, violence can also be addressed through trust, where all involved are loyal to making the school work, and where violence is perceived as a threat to such a goal. Trust may be as effective in addressing school violence as safety measures such as metal detectors, body searches, and zero-tolerance policies.

Part III

Programs

Chapter Twelve

Creating Nonviolent Schools

The previous chapters make the point that school violence involves more than school shootings or gang-related conflict. Violence is found in examples such as insults, gossiping, and intolerance for individual differences. For today's schools, violence becomes a larger social problem that goes beyond education and includes public safety, community resources, criminal justice, and the family. For example, disputes in families and communities may enter schools through the feelings and behaviors of students, where conflict is passed on to schools, rather than originating in them.

However, the origins of these conflicts may not stop the continuation of violence when they enter schools. Schools can become the "staging grounds" for increased violence, where many students have witnessed some form of crime taking place (Centers for Disease Control 2010).

The approach taken in this book states that violence goes beyond school problems to include child abuse, substance abuse, poverty, and prejudice. We believe these outside influences can be addressed through a more democratic form of school leadership. Practices such as empowerment, generosity, humor, and critical thinking are used not only within a school but also can incorporate families and communities. Schools are playing an increased role in the development of social skills for reducing school-related violence, and reducing school violence can emanate from the skill levels of those involved in the experience of schooling.

Historically, school leadership has emphasized "safety" with approaches dealing with school violence. Developing procedures that make schools safer places to learn seems an obvious conclusion, yet such measures can lead to a false sense of security. Only focusing on physical security measures sets the precedent for *evasion of these measures*, rather than prevention of the underlying reasons for violence in schools. A democratic form of leadership seeks out more long-term measures for approaching school violence through prevention, not only intervention. Creating nonviolent schools may require addressing a new approach to violence by the entire school community.

Oppression, mental illness, community gangs, and unexplainable episodes of violence by disturbed assailants become the concerns of most people involved in changing schools, but we should apply caution for overreactions to these concerns. For example, the idea that teachers should also have access to firearms in schools to counteract indescribable acts of violence seems a reactionary response that ignores most of the principles found in this book. One does not stop violent acts in schools by authorizing the potential for more violence, ignoring both safety and democratic concerns.

A democratic form of leadership works from the assumption that, in order to counteract violence, schools must establish a healthy and productive school climate. Healthy schools represent places where significant relationships are allowed to form. It may be the most effective methods for counteracting violence in schools is to work from a climate of democracy, where significant relationships are emphasized and nurtured through democratic principles. When school leaders, teachers, staff, students, families, and communities create significant relationships with each other, nonviolent schools become more of a reality.

This is a proactive approach to violence in schools, as compared to more reactive approaches such as that found in zero-tolerance policies that only focus on safety as a major concern. The following are examples of programs that promote significant relationships along with democratic methods for creating nonviolent schools.

CRISIS

Crisis intervention is on the minds of many school leaders, with the media coverage of highly visible crises such as school shootings, teen suicides, and many others. The chapter on crisis demonstrated how crises in schools can be direct and dramatic or indirect and subtle, such as in bullying. However, crisis intervention does require hands-on procedures in order for a school to resolve these events.

School leaders who focus on preparations for crisis send a message that procedures are in place and that personal safety becomes the first criteria for intervention. Some of the fundamental ingredients for resolving crisis include recognizing the early warning signals, along with practices that protect a school after a crisis is over.

Conflicts in schools have a beginning, middle, and an end, and this becomes evident in a crisis. How does a school leader know when a crisis is imminent? What does a school leader do during a crisis? How does a school leader pick up the pieces when a crisis is over? These questions can be answered by effective programs that address crisis intervention in schools. The following is one program among others that prevents crisis, and works toward creating nonviolent schools.

The Readiness and Emergency Management for Schools Technical Assistance (REMS TA) Center in Silver Spring, Maryland, was established in October 2004 by the U.S. Department of Education's Office of Safe and Healthy Students (OSHS). It represents a model depicting what is needed when crisis enters schools. This program provides the important resources when responding to crisis. The REMS TA Center disseminates information about emergency management to help schools, school districts, and institutions of higher education learn more about developing, implementing, and evaluating crisis plans.

It shares guidelines on how to sound the alarm and provide information about the event, control rumors, deal with the media, keep track of students and staff, inform parents, and interface with the community. It also addresses the aftermath of crisis with strategies that address continuation in monitoring problems, problem solving health and safety issues, and prevention planning for future crises. The REMS TA Center, along with other not-for-profit programs, help county and local school districts learn effective crisis intervention strategies.

TRAUMA

Trauma in schools historically was the responsibility of school counselors, psychologists, and other professionals trained in the effects of trauma on an individual. However, trauma in schools has another emphasis that goes beyond individual trauma. Traumatic experiences entering a school can have serious implications for the climate of a school. Changes in beliefs, traditions, and practiced skills can become altered after a significant school trauma where what was expected and practiced by school personnel is different than precrisis.

Trauma can disrupt the climate of a school to the extent that people make such comments as, "The school will never be the same after the tragic accident," or "This school was a safe place before bullying wrecked it." These are statements based on traumatic sets of circumstances influencing the climate of a school. The following example is one of many other programs that addresses trauma in schools, where consideration is given to both individual trauma and trauma affecting school climate.

A program that has directly addressed trauma in schools comes from the Massachusetts Advocate for Children in Boston, Massachusetts. Their Trauma Learning Policy Initiative, cosponsored by the Harvard Law School and the Task Force on Children Affected by Domestic Violence, has specifically addressed trauma in schools. The mission statement of this initiative is that students who were severely traumatized and have difficulty with learning are cared for in a meaningful way.

Exposure to family and other forms of violence become displaced in schools, and students can lose focus based on some traumatic incident or incidents. Issues such as difficulties with relationships, both with peers and teachers, and difficulties in controlling behavior are among other issues addressed through this initiative. This is an important program among other programs based on trauma reduction that helps in the creation of trauma-sensitive school environments.

EMOTIONS

The emotional climate found in schools cannot be ignored when it involves the impact violence has on schools. Emotions in schools are not only about each person's experience of emotions, but also the emotions experienced as a group. In the climate of a school, extreme emotional conflict can affect the beliefs, policies, and practices found in schools. Emotions such as anger, resentment, revenge, jealousy, anxiety, and apathy can change the climate of a school, when allowed to continue without any form of resolution.

In today's schools, emotions have become increasingly important, especially in maintaining an effective school climate. School policies and procedures influence the climate of a school, and the climate can shift when crisis and trauma enter schools. Furthermore, the subtle effects of emotional upheaval can devastate schools after crises have passed. The following is an example of one program among many others that addresses emotions within a school.

The National School Climate Center located in New York City makes a concerted effort to promote a positive and sustained school climate. The Center emphasizes school safety and support, and where social, ethical, academic, and emotional skills are emphasized. The Center establishes meaningful guidelines, programs, and services that support a whole school improvement model that focuses on school climate. Further emphasis is made in keeping the school climate emotionally safe, where people in schools are engaged and respected through a shared school vision (Cohen et al. 2009).

Much of the research presented through the National School Climate Center is provided by the National School Climate Council, the research arm of the Center. It has specific programs that foster collaboration between teachers, administrators, school-based mental health professionals, parents, and students. The National School Climate Center represents a national organization among more local organizations that are emphasizing emotional stability in schools. In these types of organizations, emotions of the people in the school climate are considered not only important but also represent a major focus for successfully creating a successful school climate.

EMPOWERMENT

Much of the focus in controlling violence in schools emphasizes the characteristics found in bullies, defiant students, and others who do not participate in improving school climate. A more democratic leadership style changes the focus away from dysfunctional behavior and emphasizes characteristics that empower schools, where programs that address dysfunctional behavior are complemented by those empowering a more positive school climate. The climate of a school can be seriously affected by the vision of its leaders. Constantly addressing the negative aspects found in schools changes a school's vision from "What can we do together to empower students?" to a more reactionary stance of "How do we stop violence in schools?"

Reacting only to school violence is not the direction needed when establishing the vision of a school. A more accurate question may include both aspects, namely, "How do we enact empowerment in schools while reducing school violence?" The following program is one example of answering this question. It emphasizes empowerment in the climate of a school, rather than only focusing on forceful reactions to school violence.

The Character Education Partnership is based in Washington, D.C., and is a nationally recognized program for implementing character education into the public schools. Its vision is to address young people everywhere who are educated, inspired, and empowered to be ethical and engaged citizens. Its mission is in providing the vision, leadership, and resources for schools, families, and communities in developing ethical citizens committed to building a just and caring world. One example of this program is taking place at DeSales University, where the university sponsors and judges elementary, middle, and high schools in Pennsylvania who have successfully adapted long-term character education into their curriculum (Amore 2012).

Schools across Pennsylvania are judged on such themes as caring, honesty, fairness, responsibility, and respect for self and others. Also included in character education is the use of critical-thinking skills, effective communication, skills for working together, and leadership modeling these skills to students, faculty, parents, and community. In this nationwide program, schools are empowered to focus on character with the assumption that improving the character of staff and students will improve the climate of a school. DeSales University also makes the same effort with its freshman class by offering character education to those beginning their higher education experience.

The university envisions creating character along with learning in a higher-education setting (Amore 2012). This and other examples of empowerment-oriented programs in schools attacks school violence with school empowerment by having a functional definition of one's character that does not include violence against schools.

ASSERTIVENESS

Many incidents of violence in schools are caused by how people communicate with each other. This becomes a larger problem when conflict already exists. What begins as a minor dispute can turn into physical, emotional, and psychological violence permeating the climate of a school. Communicating in an assertive manner can become the communication pattern of choice when conflict breaks out in schools. First, assertiveness can be more effective in reducing violence than creating it. Second, assertive communication is clear, proactive, and creates structure, as opposed to aggressive communication that sends mixed messages, is reactive, and breaks down the structure in schools.

Yet aggressive communication along with passive-aggressive communication (e.g., gossiping) can be found in direct and indirect forms of violence in schools. For example, physical acts of violence are, many times, accompanied by aggressive communication by the aggressor or those advocating for the aggressor, as found in aggressive gang violence. Another example is passive-aggressive communication where someone feels victimized in schools but does not communicate their feelings directly and assertively. Indirect communication develops through gossip, the spreading of rumors, or sabotage of relationships, and many other passive-aggressive communicated activities.

The following program is one example of changing aggressive communication into communication that is assertive. It is a program emphasizing assertiveness in a school climate. It advocates direct communication in order to avoid a buildup of passive-aggressive communication in schools. It looks for resolution that attacks retaliation against others who use aggressive forms of violence. The Placerville, California–based Center for Violence-Free Relationships T.E.A.C.H. (Teens Educating Against Classmate Harassment) program emphasizes youth–adult partnerships where different forms of bullying are recognized along with the development of assertiveness skills to counteract bullying behavior.

This program focuses on educating youth leaders returning to schools and becoming mentors who work to change the aggressive and passive-aggressive behavior of their peers. The T.E.A.C.H. program and many other assertiveness and bullying prevention programs offer an opportunity for schools to approach aggressive and passive-aggressive communication from a more positive perspective.

COMMON GROUND

One aspect of conflict in schools demonstrates how individuals or groups can feel isolated or polarized, and how solely relying on fact finding to understand the differences between these individuals or groups may increase potential violence, not decrease it. Many school-related conflicts need leaders who create common ground, rather than collect pertinent facts in order to render a judgment.

When people in schools realize its leaders are concerned about school unity as much as school conflict, the climate in schools adopts a different perspective regarding school-related violence. Discovering who is creating violent acts is balanced with preventing these acts from disrupting the climate of a school.

Finding common ground becomes an integral part of the climate found in more democratically oriented schools. It gives schools a balanced approach where leadership is not only perceived as being detectives, but also as being peacemakers. Programs that emphasize finding common ground create nonviolence in schools by looking for agreement and common interests, rather than separating people into categories of being acceptable and unacceptable. The subtle shift in a school's climate can be witnessed in those schools that seek common ground. The following is one of many formal programs that emphasize finding common ground in schools.

The First Amendment Center at Vanderbilt University in Nashville, Tennessee, makes a concerted effort to promote programs that emphasize the use of common ground in schools. One example is the partnership between the California County Educational Service Association and the First Amendment Center in promoting programs that counterbalance distrust and school conflict.

What is called the California Three R's—rights, responsibility, and respect—emphasizes such common ground activities in schools as creating ground rules, including all stakeholders, listening to all sides, civil debate, and following-through with proactive behavior. It reminds all stakeholders in schools that First Amendment rights need to be upheld regarding respect for each other, along with taking responsibility for each other's rights. This is a program that believes in democratic leadership and a school climate based on democratic principles.

HUMOR

Sometimes in order to make serious and difficult decisions, having a sense of humor helps expand what is possible among different factions within the climate of a school. More specifically, the climate of a school seems more equal when humor is a part of the climate. It allows both leadership and other partners in schools to meet each other beyond the roles they practice in schools. Humor is a great equalizer, where leadership can be perceived as more accessible and human when school leaders have a sense of humor.

As a point of clarification, it does not mean that so-called humor that belittles others creates equality. Humor that sends the message "We are all in this together," or "Relieving stress is a part of solving any serious problem" are examples of how humor can be used to create a democratic school climate. The use of humor in schools also helps in creating acceptance and diversity, where understanding a different subculture's perspective on humor such as racial or ethnic humor can acknowledge differences while creating empowerment and common ground in the climate of a school.

The Association of Applied and Therapeutic Humor originating in Aliso Viejo, California, has been involved in training professionals in the use of humor in many different walks of life. One of its board members, Mary Kay Morrison, specifically addresses the use of humor in her writing (Morrison 2012) and training workshops through a program called Humor Quest. Through Humor Quest, school leaders are taught the value of using humor both in leadership skills and also in the classroom.

The program points out the value found in reducing stress for those leaders who find themselves immersed in conflict and are looking for methods that use humor to improve the climate of a school. Humor Quest also points out the difference between using mockery, ridicule, bullying, and sarcasm that is taken for humor in the climate of a school. The Association of Applied and Therapeutic Humor and Humor Quest are examples of organizations and programs that recognize the use of humor both therapeutically and in the climate of a school.

CRITICAL THINKING

Controversy over the use of critical-thinking skills being taught in public schools has become both an educational and political issue. On the one side are those people who prefer not to question the beliefs of education experts, where critical thinking could possibly disrupt education rules and regulations. On the other side are those educators who believe in democracy, where questioning education rules and regulations are not only preferred but are also healthy. In creating an effective climate in schools, critical thinking requires patience, tolerance of uncertainty, and a readiness to accept the discomfort of facts that lean against one's beliefs.

In this regard, critical thinking becomes one of the goals for creating democracy in the climate of a school. It demands that schools go beyond thinking in terms of understanding facts. It requires schools to consider a commitment to analysis of information in order to obtain a comprehensive understanding of knowledge and learning. In other words, knowing information is not enough. Critical thinking asks that we know our way *around* the information through real and practiced forms of understanding.

The Center for Critical Thinking and Moral Critique in Tomales, California, acts as a research center and is a clearinghouse for information on the art of critical thinking. It supports such projects as the Critical Thinking Community that offers online streaming of critical-thinking video, online critical-thinking tests and learning tools, and an online critical-thinking library. This and other critical-thinking resources are important information-gathering sites for anyone interested in critical thinking as a part of creating a nonviolent climate within schools. Direct and indirect forms of violence mostly work from impulsive, one-dimensional thinking.

Sometimes, problems in schools are difficult to describe, especially problems focusing on violent acts. The wrong solutions can result in reactionary behavior. Critical thinking can affect everyone involved in violence by taking a proactive response to solving this problem. These types of programs offer an opportunity to network with other democratically oriented school leaders, who believe critical thinking can reduce violence in the climate of a school.

GENEROSITY

In a school climate that espouses forms of democratic leadership, the concept of generosity becomes a major component in collaborating and sharing ideas, information, and experiences with other school personnel. To be "other directed" helps change the climate of a school, and institutions that believe in generosity also believe in a climate based on collaboration, sharing, teamwork, and partnerships. Generosity in schools goes beyond funding by outside state agencies or the federal government.

It becomes an intrinsically human activity where looking beyond one's personal needs to the needs of others helps shape the climate in schools, where helping others is an expected part of everyday activity. However, creating a climate of generosity has its competitors. A school climate solely based on academic achievement can fragment the concept of generosity into unhealthy individualism and competition. Academic excellence is better served when it is shared with others. The following program is one of many that believe in generosity through collaborative efforts to help students succeed.

The National Dropout Prevention Center/Network (NDPC/N) in Clemson, North Carolina, is associated with Clemson University, and it serves as a clearinghouse on issues related to dropout prevention. It offers strategies designed to increase the graduation rate in America's schools. Over the years, the NDPC/N has become a national resource for sharing solutions for student success. Through its clearinghouse function it provides active research projects, publications, and a variety of professional development activities.

The mission of NDPC/N is to increase high school graduation rates through research and evidenced-based solutions. Since 1987, NDPC/N has worked in improving opportunities for all students to fully develop the academic, social, work, and healthy life skills needed to graduate from high school. The NDPC/N and other similar programs demonstrate the tenets found in the use of generosity in the climate of a school.

TRUST

The absence of trust in schools can keep controversy alive regarding changes made in a school, even when changes are minor, such as in who will lead the graduation ceremony. Having trust in schools has an opposite effect. Trust can be one of the primary reasons for success when instituting change. Trust also becomes important in resolving conflict. When parents, students, administrators, and teachers trust one another, the resolution of conflict is more successful and more comprehensive. Without trust, interactions between leadership and school personnel become less likely, leading to avoidance of conflict and change and increasing the chances for violence to erupt. The following program is one example among others in the use of trust to sustain a viable and productive climate in a school.

The National Education Association Foundation in Washington, D.C., partners with educators to help children learn in a conflict-ridden world. It is an organization promoting democracy in public schools through partnerships based on trust, and it includes members of the education community, parents, families, researchers, policy makers, and neighborhood communities. The NEA foundation also funds grants based on empowerment and trust, and awards educators and school leaders who practice democratic principles leading to student achievement and student development.

Though its broad base of activities focuses on more than establishing trust in schools, its vision for success encompasses many of the characteristics found in this book, including empowerment, generosity, and trust. The comprehensive scope of the NEA Foundation makes it a viable instrument for understanding and applying trust-related activities to the field of education.

References

Almeida, Leandro da Silva, and Amanda Helena Rodrigues Franco. 2011. "Critical Thinking: Its Relevance for Education in a Shifting Society." *Psicología* 29(1): 175–95.

American Psychiatric Association. 2000. *Diagnostic and Statistical Manual of Mental Health Disorders* (4th ed.). Washington, DC: American Psychiatric Association.

Amore, Gregg. 2012. "The Importance of Character Development at the University Level." *Essential Character.* Washington, DC: Character Education Partnership.

Angelle, Pamela S. 2007. "Teachers as Leaders: Collaborative Leadership for Learning Communities." *Middle School Journal 38*(3): 54–61.

Arif, Seema, and Afshan Sohail. 2009. "What Really Works in Leading a School?" *International Journal of Learning 16*(10): 695–707.

Azaiza, Khitam. 2011. "Women's Empowerment and Distance Education." *Distance Learning 8*(3): 1–4.

Bellamy, Thomas, and John I. Goodlad. 2008. "Continuity and Change in the Pursuit of a Democratic Mission for Schools." *Phi Delta Kappan 89*(8): 565.

Blanchfield, Kyle. 1983. "Developing Person-Centered Teachers." In *Freedom to Learn for the 80's*, by Carl Rogers, 180–83. Columbus, OH: Charles Merrill Publishing.

Blanchfield, Kyle E., Thomas A. Blanchfield, and Peter D. Ladd. 2008. *Conflict Resolution for Law Enforcement: Street Smart Negotiating.* Flushing, NY: Loose Leaf Law Publications.

Bloom, Gary S. 2004. "Emotionally Intelligent Principals." *School Administrator 61*(6): 14–17.

Bockler, Nils, Thorsten Seeger, Peter Sitzer, and Wilhelm Heitmeyer. 2012. *School Shootings: International Research, Case Studies and Concepts.* New York: Springer Publishing.

Bogotch, Ira. 2010. "A School Leadership Faculty Struggles for Democracy: Leadership Education Priorities for a Democratic Society." *Scholar-Practitioner Quarterly 4*(4): 378–81.

Booth-Butterfield, Melanie, and Melissa Wanzer. 2010. "Humorous Communication as Goal-Oriented Communication." In *SAGE Handbook of Communication and Instruction,* edited by Deanna Fassett and John Warren, 221–40. Thousand Oaks, CA: SAGE Publications.

Brennan, Walter. 2003. "Sounding Off about Verbal Abuse." *Occupational Health 55*(11): 22–6.

Brizendine, Bodie. 2005. "In Search of Harmony." *Independent Schools 64*(3): 94.

Browne, John R. 2012. *Walking the Equity Talk: A Guide for Culturally Courageous Leadership in School Communities.* Thousand Oaks, CA: Corwin Press.

Browne-Dianis, Judith. 2011. "Stepping Back from Zero Tolerance." *Educational Leadership 69*(1): 24.

Bryan, Julia, and Henry Lynette. 2012. "A Model for Building School-Family-Community Partnerships: Principles and Process." *Journal of Counseling & Development 90*(4): 408.

Buzwa, Eve S., Carl G. Buzwa, and Evan D. Stark. 2011. *Responding to Domestic Violence: The Integration of Criminal Justice and Human Services.* Thousand Oaks, CA: SAGE Publications.

Cantrell, Rita, Agatha Parks-Savage, and Mark Rehfuss. 2007. "Reducing Levels of Elementary School Violence with Peer Mediation." *Professional School Counseling 10*(5): 475–81.

Centers for Disease Control. 2007. "Injury Protection and Control." *Center for Disease Control* (May) http://www.cdc.gov/ViolencePrevention/data_stats/index.html.

Centers for Disease Control. 2010. "Violence Statistics." *Center for Disease Control* (October) http://www.cdc.gov/ViolencePrevention/data_stats/index.html.

Cherry, Daniel, and Jeffery M. Spiegel. 2006. *Leadership, Myth, & Metaphor: Finding Common Ground to Guide School Change.* Thousand Oaks, CA: Corwin Press.

Chhuon, Vichet, Elizabeth M. Gilkey, Margarita Gonzalez, Alan J. Daly, and Janet H. Chrispeels. 2008. "The Little District That Could: The Process of Building District-School." *Educational Administration Quarterly 44*(2): 227–81.

Chrispeels, Janet H. 2004. *Learning to Lead Together: The Promise and Challenge of Sharing Leadership.* Thousand Oaks, CA: SAGE Publications.

Cohen, Jonathan, Libby McCabe, Nicholas M. Michelli, and Terry Pickeral. 2009. "School Climate: Research, Policy, Practice, and Teacher Education." *Teachers College Record 111*(1): 180–213.

Cohen, Richard. 1999. *The School Mediator's Field Guide: Prejudice, Sexual Harassment, Large Groups & Other Challenges.* Watertown, MA: School Mediation Association.

Comer, James P., Norris M. Haynes, Edward T. Joyner, and Michael Ben-Avi. 1996. *Rallying the Whole Village: The Comer Process for Reforming Education.* New York: Teachers College Press.

Curtis, Elizabeth, and Rhona O'Connell. 2011. "Essential Leadership Skills for Motivating and Developing Staff." *Nursing Management-UK 18*(5): 32–35.

Dallas, Heather. 2011. "Assertiveness Is the Best Form of Communication." *Vital 8*(1): 36–7.

Daly, Alan J., and Janet Chrispeels. 2008. "A Question of Trust: Predictive Conditions for Adaptive and Technical Leadership in Educational Contexts." *Leadership & Policy in Schools 7*(1): 30–63.

Decker, Wayne H., and Denise M. Rotondo. 2001. "Relationships among Gender, Type of Humor, and Perceived Leader Effectiveness." *Journal of Managerial Issues 13*(4): 450.

Deford, Frank. 2012. "Budget Cuts Put School Sports on the Chopping Block." *National Public Radio,* October 6, http://www.npr.org.

Denison, Elsa. 2009. *Helping School Children: Suggestions for Efficient Cooperation with the Public Schools.* Ithaca, NY: Cornell University Press.

Dierdorff, Erich C., Eric A. Surface, and Kenneth G. Brown. 2010. "Frame-of-Reference Training Effectiveness: Effects of Goal Orientation and Self-Efficacy on Affective, Cognitive, Skill-Based, and Transfer Outcomes." *Journal of Applied Psychology 95*(6): 1181–91.

Dilulio, John. 2006. "Age of Apathy." *The Soap Box 2*(2): 9+.

Dimmock, Clive, and Allan David Walker. 2005. *Educational Leadership: Culture and Diversity.* Thousand Oaks, CA: SAGE Publications.

Doherty, Nora, and Marcelas Guyler. 2008. *The Essential Guide to Workplace Mediation and Conflict Resolution: Rebuilding Working Relationships.* London: Kogan Page Publishers.

Donaldson, Gordon A. 2006. *Cultivating Leadership in Schools: Connecting People, Purpose & Practice.* New York: Teachers College Press.

El-Ghobashy, Tamer. 2012. "Suicide Follows Secret Webcast." *Wall Street Journal* (September 10).

Evenson, Amber, Brooklyn Justinger, Elizabeth Pelischek, and Sarah Schulz. 2009. "Zero Tolerance Policies and the Public Schools: When Suspension Is no Longer Effective." *Communique 37*(5): 1.

Farenga, Patrick. 2011. "It Takes More Than a Democratic Education to Make School Meaningful to Students." *Encounter 24*(2): 28–33.

Feindler, Eva L., and Emily C. Engel. 2011. "Assessment and Intervention for Adolescents with Anger and Aggression Difficulties in School Settings." *Psychology in Schools 48*(3): 243–53.

Flemming, Kate. 2010. "Synthesis of Quantitative and Qualitative Research: An Example Using Critical Interpretive Synthesis." *Journal of Advanced Nursing 66*(1): 201–17.

Friend, Marilynn D., and Lynne Cook. 2009. *Interaction and Collaboration Skills for School Professionals.* Upper Saddle River, NJ: Pearson Publishing.

Gale, Trevor. 2011. "Social Inquiry and Social Action: Priorities for Preparing School Leaders." *Scholar Practitioner Quarterly 4*(4): 316–18.

Gardner, Deborah B. 2005. "Ten Lessons in Collaboration." *Online Journal of Issues in Nursing 10*(1): 61–74.

Gass, Robert H., and John S. Seiter. 2007. *Persuasion, Social Influence, and Compliance-Gaining*(3rd ed.). Boston: Allyn & Bacon.

Gimpel, Diane M. (2012) *The Columbine Shootings.* New York: Essential Library.

Goodwind, Melissa, and Catherine Sommervold. 2012. *Creativity, Critical Thinking and Communication: Strategies to Increase Student Skills.* Lanham, MD: Rowman & Littlefield Education.

Greenberg, Judith. 2003. *Trauma at Home: After 9/11.* New York: Bison Books.

Hammonds, Bruce. 2012. "Compliance or Creating." *Education Today* 3(5): 21–5.

Haravuori, Henna, Laura Suomalainen, Noora Berg, Olli Kiviruusu, and Mauri Marttunen. 2011. "Effects of Media Exposure on Adolescents Traumatized in a School Shooting." *Journal of Traumatic Stress 24*(1): 70–7.

Hoffman, Lori L., Cynthia J. Hutchinson, and Elayne Reiss. 2009. "On Improving School Climate: Reducing Reliance on Rewards and Punishment." *International Journal of Whole Schooling 5*(1): 1–12.

Hoffmann, Gerald D. 2009. "Applying Principles of Leadership Communication to Improve Mediation Outcomes." *Dispute Resolution Journal 64*(3): 24–9.

Hofkins, Diane. 2010. "Building a Safe, Confident Future." *Education Journal 120*: 11.

Holmes, Janet, and Meredith Marra. 2006. "Humor and Leadership Style." *Humor: International Journal of Humor Research 19*(2): 119–38.

Holt, Svetlana, and Joan Marques. 2012. "Empathy in Leadership: Appropriate or Misplaced? An Empirical Study on a Topic That Is Asking for Attention." *Journal of Business Ethics 105*: 195–205.

Hoy, Wayne K., and Richard Rees. 1974. "Subordinate Loyalty to Immediate Superior: A Neglected Concept in the Study of Educational Administration." *Sociology of Education* 47(2): 268–86.

Hurren, B. Lee. 2005. "Humor in School Is Serious Business." *International Journal of Learning 12*(6): 79–83.

Ingram, Jay, and Joseph Cangemi. 2012. "Emotions, Emotional Intelligence and Leadership: A Brief, Pragmatic Perspective." *Education 132*(4): 771–78.

Jackson-Cherry, Lisa R., and Bradley. T. Erford. 2010. *Crisis Intervention and Prevention.* Boston, MA: Pearson.

Jimerson, Shane, Amanda Nickerson, Mathew J. Mayor, and Michael J. Furlong. 2006. *Handbook of School Violence and School Safety.* Mahwah, NJ: Lawrence Erlbaum Associates.

Johnson, Karen. 2012. "Sandusky Sentenced in Penn State Sex Scandal." *USA Today*(October) http://www.usatoday.com.

Johnson, Sarah Lindstrom. 2009. "Improving the School Environment to Reduce School Violence: A Review of the Literature." *Journal of School Health 79*(10): 451–65.

Johnson, Sarah Lindstrom, Jessica Burke, and Andrea Carlson Gielen. 2012. "Urban Students' Perceptions of the School Environment's Influence on School Violence." *Children & Schools 34*(2): 92.

Jonas, Peter M. 2009. *Laughing and Learning: An Alternative to Shut Up and Listen.* Lanham, MD: Rowman & Littlefield Education.

Kafka, Judith. 2011. *The History of "Zero Tolerance" in American Public Schooling.* Hounds Mills, UK: Palgrave Macmillan.

Kaiser, Robert B., Jennifer Lindberg McGinnis, and Darren V. Overfield. 2012. "The How and the What of Leadership." *Consulting Psychology Journal: Practice and Research 64*(2): 119–35.

Kalinowski, Pav, Jerry Lai, Fiona Fidler, and Geoff Cumming. 2010. "Qualitative Research: An Essential Part of Statistical Cognition Research." *Statistics Education Research Journal* 9(2): 22–34.

Kanngiesser, Patricia, Felix Warneken, and Liane Young. 2012. "Young Children Consider Merit When Sharing Resources with Others." *Plus ONE* 7(8): 1–5.

Karp, Stan. 2008. "Undoing the Damage That Bush Leaves Behind." *Our Schools/Our Selves* 18(1): 229–43.

King, David. 2004. "Verbal Abuse . . . Assertiveness Training to Prevent Verbal Abuse." *Assertiveness Journal* 79(6): 1133.

Kirsh, Gillian A., and Nicholas A. Kuiper. 2003. "Positive and Negative Aspects of a Sense of Humor: Associations with the Constructs of Individualism and Relatedness." *Humor: International Journal of Humor Research* 16(1): 33.

Knoff, Howard M. 2012. *School Discipline, Classroom Management and Student Self- Management: A PBS Implementation Guide.* Thousand Oaks, CA: Corwin Press.

Kosmoski, Georgia, and Dennis R. Pollack. 2005. *Managing Difficult, Frustrating, and Hostile Conversations: Strategies for Savvy Administrators.* Thousand Oaks, CA: Corwin Press.

Kutsyuruba, Benjamin, Keith Walker, and Brian Noonan. 2011. "Restoring Broken Trust in the Work of School Principals." *International Studies in Educational Administration (Commonwealth Council for Educational Administration & Management [CCEAM]) 2*: 81–95.

Ladd, Peter D. 2005. *Mediation, Conciliation and Emotions: A Practitioners Guide for Understanding Emotions in Dispute Resolution.* Lanham, MD: University Press of America.

Ladd, Peter D. 2007. *Relationships and Patterns of Conflict Resolution: A Reference Book for Couples Counseling.* Lanham, MD: University Press of America.

Ladd, Peter D. 2009. *Emotional Addictions: A Reference Book for Addictions and Mental Health Counseling.* Lanham, MD: University Press of America.

Ladd, Peter D., and AnnMarie Churchill. 2012. *Person-Centered Diagnosis and Treatment in Mental Health: A Model for Empowering Clients.* London: Jessica Kingsley Publishers.

Larrivee, Barbara. 2012. *Cultivating Teacher Renewal: Guarding against Stress and Burnout.* Lanham, MD: Rowman & Littlefield Education.

Lazenby, Roland. 2007. *April 16th: Virginia Tech Remembers.* New York: Plume Publishing.

Lipman, Mathew. 2003. *Thinking in Education.* Cambridge: Cambridge University Press.

Lloyd-Smith, Laura, and Mark Baron. 2010. "Beyond Conferences: Attitudes of High School Administrators: Toward Parental Involvement in One Small Midwestern State." *School Community Journal* 20(2): 23–44.

Ludwig, Kristy A., and Jared S. Warren. 2009. "Community Violence, School-Related Protective Factors, and Psychosocial Outcomes in Urban Youth." *Psychology in the Schools* 46(10): 1061–73.

Lukaszewski, Jersey E. 2008. "The School Administrator." *Ingredients for Leadership 7(*65): 23–45.

Lynch, Rene. 2012. "Maryland School Shooting: Heroes Overpower Gunman; 1 Student Hurt." *Los Angeles Times* (August): 27.

Manasse, Lori A. 1986. "Vision and Leadership: Paying Attention to Intention." *Peabody Journal of Education 63*(1): 150–73.

Martin, David J., and Kimberly S. Loomis. 2006. *Building Teachers: A Constructivist Approach to Introducing Education.* New York: Wadsworth Publishing.

Martinez-Monteagudo, Maria C., Candido J. Ingles, M. V. Trianes, and Maria Garcia-Fernandez. 2011. "Profiles of School Anxiety: Differences in School Climate and Peer Violence." *Electronic Journal of Research in Educational Psychology 9(*3): 1023–42.

May, Rollo. 1994. *The Courage to Create.* New York: W. W. Norton & Company.

McAdams III, Charles R., and Victoria A. Foster. 2008. "Voices from 'The Front': How Student Violence Is Changing the Experience of School Leaders." *Journal of School Violence 7*(2): 87–103.

McClellan, Rhonda, and Adrienne E. Hyle. 2012. "Experiential Learning: Dissolving Classroom and Research Borders." *Journal of Experiential Education 35*(1): 238–52.

McKenry, Patrick C., and Sahara J. Price. 2005. *Families and Change: Coping with Stressful Events and Transitions.* Thousand Oaks, CA: SAGE Publishing.

McMillan Dictionaries. 2012. "Definition of Common Ground." *McMillan Dictionary.* London: MacMillan Publishing Limited.

Moore, Brooke N., and Richard Parker. 2007. *Critical Thinking* (8th ed.). New York: McGraw-Hill.

Moore, Edward H., Don H. Bagin, and Donald R. Gallagher. 2011. *The School and Community Relations.* Upper Saddle River, NJ: Pearson Publishing.

Morrison, Julie Q. 2007. "Social Validity of the Critical Incident Stress Management Model for School-Based Crisis Intervention." *Psychology in the Schools 44*(8): 765–77.

Morrison, Mary K. 2012. *Using Humor to Maximize Living: Connecting with Humor.* Lanham, MD: Rowman & Littlefield Education.

Moye, Neta A., and Claus W. Langfred. 2004. "Information Sharing and Group Conflict: Going Beyond Decision Making to Understand the Effects of Information Sharing on Group Performance." *International Journal of Conflict Management 15*(4): 381–410.

Murdach, Allison D. 2010. "What Good Is Soft Evidence?" *Social Work 55*(4): 309–16.

National Center for Education Statistics. 2007. "Compendium Report: Dropout Rates in the United States." *National Center for Education Statistics.* http://ncesedgov/pubs2007/2007059.

Newman, Catherine S., Cybelle Fox, Wendy Roth, and Jal Metha. 2005. *Rampage: The Social Roots of School Shootings.* New York: Basic Books.

Northouse, Peter G. 2012. *Leadership: Theory and Practice.* Thousand Oaks, CA: SAGE Publications.

Page, Diana, and Arup Mukherjee. 2009. "Effective Technique for Consistent Evaluation of Negotiation Skills." *Education 129*(3): 521–33.

Palestini, Robert. 2012. *No Laughing Matter: The Value of Humor in Educational Leadership.* Lanham, MD: Rowman & Littlefield Education.

Penney, Sherry H. 2011. "Voices of the Future: Leadership for the 21st Century." *Journal of Leadership Studies 5*(3): 55–62.

Pepper, Kay, and Lisa H. Thomas. 2002. "Making Change: The Effects of the Leadership Role on School Climate." *Learning Environments Research 5*(2): 155–66.

Rashid, Faaiza, and Amy Edmondson. 2012. "Risky Trust: How Teams Build Trust Despite High Risk." *Rotman Magazine*: 55–59.

Reback, Randall. 2010. "Schools' Mental Health Services and Young Children's Emotions, Behavior, and Learning." *Journal of Policy Analysis and Management 29*(4): 698–725.

Reidel, Michelle, and Cinthia Salinas. 2011. "The Role of Emotion in Democratic Dialogue: A Self-Study." *Social Studies Research & Practice 6*(1): 2–20.

Richardson, Michael D., Kenneth E. Lane, and Jackson L. Flanigan. 1995. *School Empowerment.* Lanham, MD: Rowman & Littlefield Education.

Roberts, Josh K. 2011. "Internet Defamation: Defending Your Name." *Forensic Examiner*: 19–21.

Rogers, Carl. 1983. *Freedom to Learn for the 80's.* Columbus, OH: Charles Merrill Publishing.

Rubinkam, Michael. 2012. "Jerry Sandusky to Be Sentenced Oct. 9 in Penn State Sex Abuse Case." *Hufffington Post* (October), http://www.huffingtonpost.com.

Rustin, Michael, and David Armstrong. 2012. "What Happened to Democratic Leadership?" *Soundings 13*(50): 59–71.

Ryan, James, and Cindy Rottmann. 2009. "Struggling for Democracy: Administrative Communication in a Diverse School Context." *Educational Management Administration & Leadership 37*(4): 473–96.

Saltmarsh, Sue, Kerry Robinson, and Cristyn Davies. 2012. *Rethinking School Violence: Theory, Gender, Context.* Hampshire, UK: Palgrave McMillan.

Schwab, Gabrielle. 2010. *Haunting Legacies: Violent Histories and Trans-Generational Trauma.* New York: Columbia University Press.

Shaker, Erika. 2010. "In Defense of Failure." *Our Schools/Our Selves 19*(2): 27–31.

Shariff, Shaheen S. 2009. *Confronting Cyber-Bullying: What Schools Need to Know to Control Misconduct and Avoid Legal Consequences.* Cambridge, UK: Cambridge University Press.

Shouppe, Gary, and James L. Pate. 2010. "Teachers' Perceptions of School Climate, Principal Leadership Style and Teacher Behaviors on Student Academic Achievement." *National Teacher Education Journal 3*(2): 87–98.

Siddique, Anam, Hasan D. Aslam, Mannam Khan, and Urooj Fatima. 2011. "Impact of Academic Leadership on Faculty's Motivation and Organizational Effectiveness in Higher Education System. *International Journal of Academic Research 3*(3): 730–37.

Siddiqui, Sahid. 2011. "Educational Leadership: Change through Self-Understanding." *Bulletin of Education & Research 33*(1): 21–29.

Simplicio, Joseph 2011. "It All Starts at the Top: Divergent Leadership Styles and their Impact upon a University." *Education 132*(1): 110.

Sleegers, Peter, Hartger Wassink, Klass van Veen, and Joreon Imants. 2009. "School Leaders' Problem Framing: A Sense-Making Approach to Problem-Solving Processes of Beginning School Leaders." *Leadership & Policy in Schools 8*(2): 152–72.

Smith, Carolyn A., Allan Lizotte, Terrance Thornberry, and Marvin Krohn. 1996. "Resilient Youth: Identifying Factors That Prevent High-Risk Youth from Engaging in Delinquency and Drug Use." In *Delinquency and Disrepute in the Life Course*, edited by James Hagen, 217–47. Greenwich, CT: JAI Press.

Smith, Douglas C., and Daya S. Sandhu. 2004. "Toward a Positive Perspective to Violence Prevention in Schools: Building Connections." *Journal of Counseling & Development 82*(4): 287–93.

Stanovich, Keith E., and Richard F. West. 2008. "On the Failure of Cognitive Ability to Predict My Side and One-Sided Thinking Biases." *Thinking & Reasoning 14*(2): 129–67.

Starr, Lisa J. 2010. "An Examination of Tension in the Space between Leadership Philosophy and the Cultural Reality of Schools." *Academic Leadership 8*(4): 43.

Stewart, Charlotte G., and William A. Lewis. 1986. "Effects of Assertiveness Training on the Self-Esteem of Black High School Students." *Journal of Counseling & Development 64*(10): 638.

Thiederman, Sondra. 2004. "How to Achieve Bias-Free Leadership." *Journal for Quality & Participation 27*(4): 5–8.

Treasurer, Bill. 2011. "Leadership's First Virtue: Be Courageous." *School Administrator 68*(8): 28–31.

Tyack, David. 2007. *Seeking Common Ground: Public Schools in a Diverse Society.* Cambridge, MA: Harvard University Press.

Underwood, Doug. 2011. *Chronicling Trauma: Journalists and Writers on Violence and Loss.* Chicago: University of Illinois Press.

U.S. Department of Education. 2011. *The Handbook for Campus Safety and Security Reporting.* Washington, DC: U.S. Department of Education, http://www2.ed.gov.

U.S. Department of Justice. 2012. *Causes of School Violence.* Washington, DC: U.S. Department of Justice.

Vlieghe, Joris, Maartens Simons, and Jan Masschelein. 2010. "The Educational Meaning of Communal Laughter: On the Experience of Corporeal Democracy." *Educational Theory 60*(6): 719–34.

Vryonides, Marios. 2007. "Struggling between Traditional and Modernity: Gender and Education Choice-Making." *Gender in Education 19*(1): 93–107.

Waldron, Nancy L., James McLeskey, and Lacy Redd. 2011. "Setting the Direction: The Role of the Principal in Developing an Effective, Inclusive School." *Journal of Special Education Leadership 24*(2): 51–60.

Wildman, Beth G., and Brett Clementz. 1986. "Assertive, Empathic Assertive, and Conversational Behavior." *Behavior Modification 10*(3): 315.

Zahrani, Abdul A. 2012. "Psychological Empowerment and Workplace Learning: An Empirical Study of Saudi Telecom Company." *Advances in Management 5*(2): 37–46.

Ziv, Avner. 1988. "The Teacher's Sense of Humor and the Atmosphere in the Classroom." *School Psychology International 1*: 21–23.

Index

About the Authors

Kyle Elizabeth Blanchfield, JD, is president and CEO of the Northern New York Centers for Conflict Resolution, which cover the entire northern region of New York State. She served as the former president of the New York State Dispute Resolution Association and also as a former justice court judge. She is an adjunct assistant professor of education in St. Lawrence University's Graduate Leadership Program. She teaches education law, conflict resolution, leadership and school violence, and leadership and school climate.

Peter D. Ladd, PhD, has been a tenured faculty member at St. Lawrence University in the Graduate School of Education for over thirty years. He coordinates the Certificate of Advanced Studies Program in counseling, and has worked for thirty-five years in St. Lawrence University's satellite graduate school program on the Akwesasne Mohawk Reservation. He has written numerous books on conflict resolution, mental health counseling, addictions counseling, marriage and family counseling, and Aboriginal studies.